当代语言学研究文库

LINGUISTICS

汉语句首受事话题的句法与语篇研究

Syntactic and Discoursal Dimentions of Clause-initial Patient Topics in Mandarin Chinese

童剑平 著

上海交通大学出版社
SHANGHAI JIAO TONG UNIVERSITY PRESS

内 容 提 要

本书对汉语自然口语中句首受事话题进行实证性研究。全书由七章组成。第一章为导言，简要介绍本书的研究范围、研究问题以及研究意义和本书结构。第二章是文献综述，对以往关于汉语话题的句法特征、话题分类、话题结构以及话题语篇功能的理论加以评介。第三章描述本书的研究方法。第四章研究充当句首受事话题的语类。第五章研究句首受事话题句句式类型和英译。第六章研究句首受事话题的语篇关联。第七章为结论。本书系统地将句首受事话题的研究从句法层面扩展到语篇层面，将这类话题的形式与功能研究有机地结合起来，对已有的相关研究具有补充作用，对汉语中其他类型话题的研究可提供借鉴。

本书适合对汉英对比研究感兴趣的读者以及高等院校语言文学学科的教师和学生阅读。

图书在版编目(CIP)数据

汉语句首受事话题的句法与语篇研究/童剑平著.
—上海：上海交通大学出版社，2013
（当代语言学研究文库）
ISBN 978-7-313-10041-2

Ⅰ. 汉...　Ⅱ. 童...　Ⅲ. 汉语—口语—研究
Ⅳ. H193.2

中国版本图书馆 CIP 数据核字(2013)第 148025 号

汉语句首受事话题的句法与语篇研究
童剑平　著
上海交通大学出版社出版发行
（上海市番禺路 951 号　邮政编码 200030）
电话：64071208　出版人：韩建民
凤凰数码印务有限公司 印刷　全国新华书店经销
开本：787mm×960mm 1/16　印张：11.75　字数：218 千字
2013 年 9 月第 1 版　2013 年 9 月第 1 次印刷
ISBN 978-7-313-10041-2/H　定价：32.00 元

前言

国外学者 Li and Thompson(1976)从功能主义出发,以话题突出与否和主语突出与否作为语言分类标准提出,汉语属于话题突出型(topic-prominent)语言,英语属于主语突出型(subject-prominent)语言。这一观点已被广泛接受。随着国内外研究者们不断地对汉语话题进行多视角的探索,汉语话题已经成为国际语言学界共同探讨的课题之一,其性质也越来越为人们所认识。汉语里多种语类可以充当话题,即话题化。Xu and Langendoen(1985)认为,可以充当话题的主要语类有名词短语(包括量词短语)、分句、话题化分句、动词短语、前置词短语以及后置词短语。从话题与述题或述题中某一成分语义关系出发,徐烈炯、刘丹青(1998)把汉语话题分为论元及准论元共指性、语域式、拷贝式以及分句式话题四大类。这些关于话题分类的思想在理论上具有开创性意义,但在汉语话题的深入、细化研究方面,它们的解释力存在较大局限性。在充当句首受事话题的语类成分中,哪些语类成分是无标记、典型的?哪些语类成分是有标记、非典型的?受事话题结构都有哪些句式类型?哪些是无标记的?哪些有标记的?此外,一个句式的选择与语境因素密切相关。话题具有语篇特征,这已是研究者们的共识。然而句首受事话题是如何实现语篇功能的?现有的研究对这些问题尚不能提供有效的解答。

本书以句首受事话题为切入点,试图对上述问题做出回答。句首受事话题是论元共指性话题的一种,就句法表现而言,与充当次话题的受事话题不同(后者位于句子主语和谓语动词之间)。在本书中,句首受事话题的可操作性定义是,位于句首或接近句首、与述题中主要动词或相关动词后的空位共指、并通过空位成为支配性动词内部论元的话题化成分。这类话题广义上是动作行为的承受者、目标、对象、处所、工具、产物和心理活动涉及的事件、状态等,其前或后可以有话题标记,其后可以有停顿。句首受事话题句指包含句首受事话题的结构。句首受事话题语篇截段指含有句首受事话题句的语段。每个语篇截段中包含 9 个小句——1 个受事话题句,8 个语境句。受事话题句处于 8 个语境句的中间位置,即受事话题句的左、右侧分别排列有 4 个连续的语境句。话题或话题中的成分与某一语境句中相关成分具有语义连接,借此建立与该语境句的关联,这种关联在本书中称为句首受事话题的语篇关联。

本书从 33 个(时间总长度约为 1,052 分钟,平均长度约为 32 分钟)访谈、叙述、讲座、对话等形式的自然口语类电视节目的录音或录像文件中收集语料,获取 217 个句首受事话题句和含有这些话题句的 217 个语篇截段(共计 1,953 个小句),转写后输入计算机,分别建立小型封闭式单语语料库和子库。

本书的研究发现主要有以下三个方面:

(1) 可以充当句首受事话题的语类有名词短语、指示词、内嵌小句、同位结构、量词短语和动词短语。这些语类在语料中的分布是不均匀的,按出现的频率,呈名词短语>指示词>内嵌小句>同位结构>量词短语>动词短语的等级排列顺序。名词短语在语料中的出现频率最高,是无标记、典型语类。量词短语和动词短语在语料中的出现极少,是有标记、非典型语类。在话题化的名词短语中,简单名词短语的出现频数远远大于复杂名词短语的出现频数,是无标记、典型的次语类,复杂名词短语是有标记、非典型的次语类。无标记语类/次语类与有标记语类/次语类话题在指称属性、参与者角色或认知特征方面存在着差异。

(2) 句首受事话题句共有三大类、27 种句式。其中 TSV 和 TV 的出现频率远远超过其他句式,是典型句首受事话题句句式。以 Gregory and Michaelis(2001)对英语口语中话题化的研究为参照进行汉英对比显示,汉语中 TSV 句式的出现频率与英语中 OSV 句式的出现频率相比,按每分钟实例出现频数计算,前者约是后者的 1.63 倍。对两部汉语话剧文本《茶馆》和《狗儿爷涅磐》进行穷尽性调查,结果显示,其中受事话题句句式分布情况与自然口语中不尽相同。在 115 例话题句中,仅有 7 种句式,句式类型远不及自然口语中丰富。语料中出现频率最高的句式是 TV,远超 TSV,成为使用最多的、典型的句首受事话题句句式。TSV 降级为非典型句首受事话题句句式。进一步研究 115 例受事话题句的英译发现,SVO 为句首受事话题句的主要译文形式,OSV 的使用为

4 例。将原文中 TSV 的频率与译文中 OSV 的频率相比较，前者是后者的 8.25 倍，大于汉语句首受事话题句的频率与英语话题化的频率在口语中的差别。这表明，OSV 转换形式在上述话剧文本英译中的使用处于偏离自然状态的过低程度。从功能角度出发，本书揭示了这样一个悖论，即受事话题的语篇关联特征及其非焦点信息状态并不能在 SVO 这一普遍使用的译文形式中得到同等程度的再现。

（3）本书在词汇衔接（Halliday and Hasan 1976）、词汇重复（Hoey 1991）和统称词的指同意义（廖秋忠 1986）等理论框架下，对句首受事话题的语篇关联方式进行调查，并建立模型。结果显示，双侧关联是这类话题的典型语篇关联方式，而单纯左侧或右侧关联则是非典型语篇关联方式。双侧均无关联的话题在语料库中极少。此外，与受事话题关联的语境句出现在话题结构左侧的频率大于出现在其右侧的频率。受事话题的语篇关联程度与所关联的小句的位置密切相关。统计结果显示，在语篇截段中，关联语境句的出现频率在靠近话题结构的位置上较高，在远离话题结构的位置上则相对较低。受事话题的语篇关联模式与信息处理的快速、省力认知特征相符合。

本书从小处着眼，透过句首受事话题这一微观现象，对其形式和功能特征进行深入、细化的探索，旨在为汉语话题的总体研究开辟一条新途径，为其他类别话题的研究提供有效的参考。

英汉缩略语对照表

AP	apposition	同位语
CIP topic	clause-initial patient topic	句首受事话题
cit	citation	引用语
CP/cp	classifier phrase	量词短语
CIPT clause	clause-initial patient topic clause	句首受事话题句
DEM	demonstrative	指示词
det	determiner	限定词
EC/ec	embedded clause	内嵌句/嵌套句
ex-q	existential quantifier	存在量词
g-q	generic quantifier	类指数量词
ind	indefinite pronoun	不定代词
L/l	leftward	左向的
MC	matrix clause	母句
mod	modifier	修饰语
NP/np	noun phrase	名词短语
OSV	object-subject-verb	宾语-主语-动词
pos	possessive	领属词
prop	proper noun	专有名词
R/r	rightward	右向的
SL	source language	源语
T	topic	话题
TL	target language	目的语
TOP	topicalisation	话题化
TSV	topic-subject-verb	话题-主语-动词
TV	topic-verb	话题-动词
uni-q	universal quantifier	全称量词
VP	verb phrase	动词短语

英汉符号对照表

∨	intra-utterance pause	话语内停顿
∈	belong to	属于
∉	not belong to	不属于
⊂	be included in	真包含于
∩	intersection	交
∪	union	并
⟷	equivalence	对应
∨	or	或
∧	and	和
≫	presuppose	预设
≤	poset/partially ordered set	偏序集

Contents

List of tables

1

List of figures

Chapter 1   Introduction

Ample research has been conducted on clause topics in Chinese ever since Chao (1968/1979:45) proposed that it is more appropriate to treat subject and predicate in Chinese as topic and comment in that subject-predicate clauses, if the subject is an actor, account for at most about half of all clauses. Li and Thompson's (1976) widely accepted view that Chinese is a topic-prominent language while English is a subject-prominent language has further added impetus into investigation in this area. Clause topic as a syntactic phenomenon has attracted broad attention from different stances and its properties gradually come to light with plentiful studies being published. Nonetheless, the features of clause topic are on no account understood adequately or thoroughly. Different types of clause topics have been identified in Chinese. Yet, not much in-depth research has been carried out on a specific type or extended to explore its discourse functions from an empirical perspective though the idea has been proposed repeatedly that clause topics possess discourse properties. This is where the current study is set out. Drawing on previous studies, this book is intended to be a unique probe of its type, for the author of the book is convinced that concentrating on one particular type of topics is essential and worthwhile, if we expect in real earnest to gain a full and insightful picture of the features of those topics, rather than tackling all types of topics en masse without giving them separate treatment and thus leaving type-specific features still veiled.

1.1 Scope of the study

From the angle of syntax, Xu and Langendeon (1985) identify clause topics as coming under six major categories, namely, NP (including quantifier phrases as a special case), S, S', VP, PrepP (prepositional phrase) and PostP (postpositional phrase). More than a decade later, taking semantic factors into consideration, Xu and Liu (1998) reclassify clause topics into four types as argument and quasi-

1

argument co-reference topics, domain topics, copy topics and clause topics①. Each of the four types can be subdivided in one way or another. In Xu and Liu's classification, semantic relation is taken into account that holds between the topic and comment or an item contained in the comment within a topic structure. In this book, the author follows Xu and Liu's classification and focuses on one sub-type of argument and quasi-argument co-reference topics: clause-initial patient topics, shortened as CIP topics. The study is not limited to the topics, though. The syntactic types of clauses that contain a CIP topic, i. e. clause-initial patient topic clauses, shortened as CIPT clauses, are also probed into. Moreover, it will extend to cover discoursal associations of the topics in question.

Based on the definition of CIP topics given by Xu and Liu (1998:250), an operational definition of CIP topics adopted in this study is:

(1) A CIP topic is a topicalized constituent within a clause that occupies the initial or near-initial position. It is coreferential with a gap behind a verb in the comment no matter whether the verb is a matrix one or not and thus forms the internal argument of that verb through the gap.

The instance below from the autor's corpus data is an illustration of the definition.

(2) 这个债你得还/②,③

Example (2) is a typical CIPT clause in which the demonstrative noun phrase "这个债" is a CIP topic. It has a definite reference to something mentioned earlier and is coreferential with the gap behind the verb "还". The topicalized noun phrase hence forms the internal argument of "还". The agent "你" of the predicate verb plays the grammatical role of subject in the clause. Though a CIP topic is termed as

---

① Xu and Liu's works is published in Chinese. The types of clause topics in their classification are translated by the author.

② Examples used in the present study are mainly taken from the corpus created by the author for the purpose of the present study and will not be stated specifically later. When other scholars' examples are cited, illustrations will be given.

③ The slash symbol "/" rather than the punctuation mark "," or "。" is employed throughout this book to indicate the end of a clause.

"patient topic", the semantic role that it fulfills is not necessarily confined to "patient". In a broad sense, topics of this type might be patient, recipient, goal, location, tool or product in relation to the activity a verb describes. They might as well be an event or state of affairs involved in a psychological activity. In this case, a CIP topic is realized by an embedded clause. Consider:

(3) 我后面是谁我没去看/

In example (3), the embedded clause "我后面是谁" is topicalized and coreferential with the gap behind the matrix verb "看". It forms the internal argument of "看" and thus a CIP topic. The pronoun "我" in boldface plays the grammatical role of subject in the CIPT structure.

Cases where the grammatical subject does not occur are quite common. Consider:

(4) a. 秦可卿的丧事都办完了/
    b. 音乐奏起来了 (Chen 1986:58)
    c. 僵局终于打破了 (Liu 2002:265)
    d. 小李撞伤了 (Fan 1998:167)
    e. 橘子苹果买了一大堆 (Pan 1997:365)
    f. 三军之事乎不与谋 (*Zuo Zhuan* Duke Ai, 9th Year)

The six clauses in example (4) are of the same syntactic construction. (4a) is from my corpus and treated as a CIPT clause. (4b~4f) are interpreted by different scholars in different ways, though. For Chen, example (4b) equals a clause in which an agent marker like "被" is used and is in essence a passive clause. Liu perceives (4c) as an implicit passive clause in that both the agent and the preposition "被" introducing the agent are dropped. Under Fan's view, however, clause (4d) is a descriptive clause rather than a passive clause. The initial noun phrase "小李" is the clause topic and the verb phrase "撞伤了" is the comment. The constitute "撞伤了" simply describes the state of affairs that "小李" is in. Pan holds that it is more appropriate to interpret (4e) as a topic structure. Diachronically, the construction is used even in ancient Chinese. Instance (4f) is taken from the ancient Chinese classic *Zuo Zhuan*. In the eyes of Shen (1986),

"三军之事" is a clause topic coreferential with the gap succeeding the predicate verb "谋". Ideas of Fan, Pan and Shen jointly provide a good basis for the treatment of (4a) as a CIPT clause in the present study. In this example, the initial noun phrase "秦可卿的丧事" is a CIP topic and coreferential with the gap behind the verb phrase "办完". It forms the patient argument of "办完". The agent of the verb "办", also the subject of the clause, is omitted for brevity since its referent has already been mentioned in the previous discourse. It needs to be pointed out that passive clauses are not included in this study anyway. If a passive preposition such as "被", "给", "叫" or "让" is used in a clause, no matter whether it is followed by an agent or not, the clause is not treated as a CIPT clause. On the other hand, if neither a passive preposition is used nor the agent argument occurs, a clause having the same construction as (4a) is identified as a felicitous CIPT clause.

Sometimes the position a CIP topic occupies is not literally initial but near-initial. Consider:

(5) 每天大概二、三十块钱也能挣得到/

Example (5) resembles (4a) in that the subject, also the agent argument, is omitted. Where the two clauses differ from each other is that example (5) contains two clause topics: the initial time element "每天" and the near-initial noun phrase "大概二、三十块钱". The former is a domain topic—establishing a time frame while the latter a CIP topic, coreferential with the gap behind the verb phrase "挣得到" and governed by it. Example (5) qualifies as a topic structure with double main topics. Such a claim is in accordance with Xu and Liu's (1998:58) view that a topic structure may contain several main topics as long as they precede the first non-topic element.

Other CIPT clauses differ from the above in one way or another. Consider:

(6) 我觉得[这个事情我真的不想去做]/
(7) (这个)[元春](呢)ⱽ小说就告诉你[就选进去了]/①

---

① The symbol "ⱽ" is used to mark an intra-clause pause.

In both examples above, the parts in boldface are matrix clauses. The parts enclosed by the square brackets are CIPT clauses embedded within the matrix clauses and function as internal argument of the relevant matrix verb. The italicized items "这个事情" and "元春" are both CIP topics. In (6), the topicalized noun phrase "这个事情" occupies the initial position of the embedded clause. In (7), however, the topicalized proper noun "元春" occupies the near-initial position preceding the matrix clause and stands away from the comment it goes with. The bracketed element "这个……呢" is a compound topic marker.

Some CIPT clauses deserve special attention when they contain *shi*... *de* construction, or they will be dismissed unintentionally. The *shi*... *de* construction is more frequently used in spoken Mandarin than in written Chinese. Generally speaking, its occurrence may affect the syntactic pattern of a clause but not the semantic pattern. Compare the pair in (8):

(8) a. 两本书我同时写。
     b. 两本书是同时写的/

Example (8a) is a clause that one can easily invent by intuition. Example (8b) is taken from my corpus. The two clauses are different syntactically. The initial noun phrase "两本书" in (8a) is a standard CIP topic. The pronoun "我" is the subject. The verb "写" is a two-place predicate. "两本书" binds the empty position succeeding "写" and is governed by it. Drawing on Zhu (1982:105), "两本书" in (8b) can be analysed as the subject. The copula "是" is the predicate. The element "同时写的" is the object. However, if "是" is dropped here, the resultant clause is still well-formed and the semantic structure will not change. In this sense, "是" is optional. In the present study, "两本书" is identified as CIP topic as well as subject. The agent argument of the verb "写" is dropped. Unlike its counterpart in (8a), "两本书" in this case has no way to be put back. Nonetheless, it is still governed by the verb "写" and holds a coreferential relationship with the post-verbal gap. Consider another example:

(9) 这个木料原来是谁订的货呀/

Instance (9) is a very unusual case. The copula "是" plays the role of predicate.

It functions to link the two constituents that appear before and after it. The subject and topic coincide, realized by the noun phrase "这个木料". The grammatical role of object of the clause is played by the noun phrase "谁订的货". In essence, it is the object that induces the divergence between example (8b) and (9). Here within the objective noun phrase, "货" is the head modified by the *de* phrase "谁订的" that functions as a relative clause. "订" is a two-place verb taking two arguments. In this case, the interrogative word "谁" occurs as the agent argument of the verb "订". As for its patient argument, there are two candidates: the topicalized noun phrase "这个木料" and its superordinate noun "货". The former is considered a better choice than the latter. One reason is that "这个木料", as the topic of the clause, should be treated as more closely related to the verb "订" in the comment if the claim is held to be valid that the comment in an information structure is something said about the topic. Another reason is that the head of the objective noun phrase "货" is not obligatory in the clause. If "货" is omitted, the clause still stands acceptable without any change in meaning. An alternative way of analyzing the initial noun phrase "这个木料" is applicable when the idea of "governing through transmission" (Lu and Shen 2003:232) is followed. Namely, if "货" is considered being governed by "订", then "这个木料", as a hyponym item of "货", is governed by "订" through transmission. No matter how it is analyzed, there are good grounds for treating "这个木料" as a CIP topic. Intuitively, clauses similar to (8b) are more common than clauses similar to (9) in spoken Chinese. This intuition will be proved to be true later in the phase of syntactic investigation in this study.

Once in a while a verb phrase can be topicalized. Consider example (10) below:

(10) 量房子我不可能不知道/

The initial verb phrase "量房子" is coreferential with the gap succeeding the matrix verb "知道" in the comment. Literally, it does not encode a participant engaged in the activity "知道" describes. Yet, when the verb phrase "量房子" in TOP is perceived as equivalent to an embedded clause in which the subject is elliptic because it has an antecedent in the previous discourse or its referent is inferable in the context, it can be treated as denoting an event and ideationally forms the internal argument or para-internal argument of the verb "知道". Accordingly, it is considered a CIP topic or para-CIP topic.

Detailed discussion of syntactic patterns of CIPT clauses will be made later in chapter 5. In short, CIPT clauses do not exhibit one uniform syntactic pattern but diverse patterns—some are typical and some non-typical. The attempt made to take as many different patterns as possible into account in this book is deemed to be conducive to the research on CIP topics in a wider scope and therefore to a fuller understanding of them. Undoubtedly, the more the syntactic patterns are captured, the more CIP topics will be obtained and the more reliable the descriptions will be.

The definition of CIP topic given previously in (1) excludes instances in which the topicalized constituent is coreferential with a post-verbal element. Consider:

(11) 吴先生, 我认识[他]。Xu and Liu (1998:123)

(12) 赚大钱, 我可不指望[这样的事]。(ibid)

According to Xu and Liu, in (11), the topic "吴先生" and the bracketed pronoun "他" in the comment are in a binding relation or co-indexing relation. In other words, the topic binds the co-indexed element in the comment. In (12), the topic, embodied by the verb phrase "赚大钱", and the bracketed noun phrase "这样的事" are in a binding relation. The co-indexed elements in both (11) and (12) can be elliptic without changing the meanings of the clauses. Instances like (11) and (12), where the co-indexed elements are not elliptic, are left-dislocations in nature. No matter whether the co-indexed elements are elliptic or not, in the eyes of Xu and Liu, both "吴先生" and "赚大钱" are argument co-reference topics. Left-dislocation merits an independent study since topicalization and left-dislocation differ in many ways. Diverging from Xu and Liu, cases like (11) and (12), i. e., left dislocations, are not covered in the present study.

Yuan (1996) notices that a preverbal noun phrase may be governed by a verb that does not syntactically occur. Such a case is encountered in this study. Consider:

(13) a. 外语你得下功夫[学]。(ibid)

b. 你对你父亲做的你觉得也是应该[做]的/

Example (13a) is cited from Yuan whereas (13b) is an instance from my own corpus. The verbs in brackets are unexpressed but can be added according to the context. The initial noun phrase "外语" in (13a) is not related to the verb phrase "下功夫". Rather, it is, as Yuan points out, semantically governed by the covert verb "学". By the same token, the *de* structure "你对你父亲做的" in (13b) can be treated as being semantically governed by the covert content verb "做" and forming its internal argument. Thus, (13b) is identified as a CIPT clause.

A discoursal dimension of CIP topics displays how the elements functionally behave and what precise traits they possess therein.

The perspective of this corpus-based study is empirical. Both qualitative and quantitative examinations are involved. Qualitative analyses are made in the phases of data collection, data coding and discussion of results whereas quantitative analyses are made when the corpus data are statistically dealt with. Different from many researchers who mainly conduct their investigations into invented data or data drawn from written discourse, naturally occurring spoken data collected by myself are employed as the grounds of argument in the current study since I believe that spoken language provides a better guide to the understanding of CIP topics and that the features of these syntactic constituents show up more clearly and naturally in authentic communication.

1.2　Research questions

The syntactic and discoursal approach of this book to CIP topics involves addressing research questions as follows.

(1) What categories and subcategories of linguistic units can fulfill the syntactic role of CIP topic and how do they distribute in the spoken data?

(2) What syntactic patterns do CIPT clauses exhibit? And how do the patterns distribute?

(3) In what ways are CIP topics or elements contained in them discoursally associated with contextual clauses on both sides of topic structures within the scope of discourse chunks? And what patterns do the

8

associations typically display?

Each of the questions above forms a major aspect of the study and leads to further pursuit of relevant specific questions.

1.3 Significance of the study

Taking such factors as phrasal category and semantic role into account, the present study empirically explores CIP topics in Mandarin Chinese from both syntactic and discoursal perspectives. The findings are original and have important implications for relevant studies on other types of topics.

For a start, this study sets out to investigate categories of linguistic forms in their capacity as CIP topics. Xu and Langendoen (1985) believe that six major categories of linguistic units can appear in TOP: NP (including quantifier phrases as a special case), S, S', VP, PrepP (prepositional phrase) and PostP (postpositional phrase). Targeting at clause topics as a whole, such a claim cannot be assumed to apply to each individual type of topics though it exhibits considerable explanatory power. Moreover, S and S', due to their syntactic variation, are viewed by these scholars as forming separate categories. Consider the following instances used by Xu and Langendoen (ibid):

(14) *Ta hui shuo zhexie hua* wo bu xiangxin.

"That he could have said these words, I don't believe."

(15) *zhexie hua Ta hui shuo* wo bu xiangxin.

"That these words he could have said, I don't believe."

In Xu and Langendoen, the embedded clause in TOP in (14)—the italicized part—is analyzed as S while that in (15) as S', a distinct category. From my point of view, the embedded clause in (15), a topic structure itself, is just a syntactic variation of the embedded clause in (14). Though syntactically divergent from its counterpart in (14), the topicalized constituent in (15) does not seem to merit a separate categorical identification in any way. To avoid flawed categorization like this and to see exactly what categories of linguistic forms can occur in TOP, the present study chooses to combine semantic and syntactic factors and to focus on one specific type of clause topics, namely, CIP topics rather than on all types of topics mixed together without distinction. The description is thus type-specific.

Second, the syntax[1] of CIPT clauses is approached categorically from a broader perspective. In the past, when CIP topics being touched upon, attention was mainly focused on the rather standard pattern of topic structures like aforementioned example (2) in which the subject occurs. Other structures in which the subject does not occur as in example (4) and (5) or structures in which the *shi...de* construction or its variation is used are for the most part not taken into account. In this book, more syntactic types of CIPT clauses are covered and discussed.

Third, a functional approach to CIP topics is adopted in two ways. One is that based on naturally occurring data instead of introspective or intuitive data, the study examines CIP topics in use. In this sense, the present study has the significance of supplementing the previous studies in that it provides a truer view of linguistic units playing the role of CIP topic. The other is that taking CIP topics as a point of departure, this book then proceeds to the investigation of their discoursal associations. There has been consensus in the literature about discourse properties of topics. Such properties, however, have been neither delved into empirically nor described in detail. This study explores the syntactic phenomenon in relation to its discourse function. Put precisely, the study probes into distributions of both leftward and rightward contextual clauses with which CIP topics or elements contained in the topics are discoursally associated. The findings therefore specifically depict the frequently mentioned discourse properties on the part of CIP topics and provide a remedy for Tsao's (1977/1995) view that topics reveal discourse features by means of being "relating", "introductory" or "chaining". In this sense the present study forms an extension of Tsao's idea.

In the main, this book examines CIP topics while taking semantic, syntactic and discoursal factors all into account. Such an effort proves to be instrumental and rewarding in that a deeper insight into the phenomenon will be acquired. Understandings obtained therein are hopefully constructive to the studies of other types of clause topics in Mandarin Chinese.

---

① What is meant by syntax in this book has nothing to do with the controversial issue of the formation of CIP topics—whether they are derived or basic. It simply refers to the syntactic categorization of CIPT clauses. In other words, the plausible syntactic patterns of CIPT clauses are to be investigated.

1.4 Outline of the study

As shown in many previous studies (Li and Thompson 1976; Xu and Langendoen 1985; Yuan 1996; Shi 2000), a discussion of clause topics is often inevitably intertwined with a discussion of topic structures. This is also true with the present study. In the author's attempt to gain an overall understanding of CIP topics, the research, naturally enough, starts with probing into categories of units functioning as CIP topics and their distributions in the corpus data, and ends up with investigating the distributional patterns of discoursal associations on the part of these topics. Practically, the attempt requires that the examination of CIP topics not be separated from the examination of the clause structures in which the topics are embraced. To a certain extent, the latter examination process occurs even earlier than the former when topicalized utterances are picked from the recording samples in the stage of data collection. The fact that CIPT clauses exhibit great syntactic diversity is very striking and impressive. Relevant studies in this regard are, unfortunately, so scanty and deficient that I just feel I cannot turn a blind eye to the phenomenon and leave it unexplained. This results in the inclusion, in the book, of a part devoted to the syntax of topic structures. The part is positioned between the two parts—one dealing with phrasal categories of CIP topics and the other with their discoursal associations—for the sake of an arrangement that the discussion proceeds in a micro to macro manner in the study.

The book is structured in the same way as most empirical studies. Chapter 1 is introductory in which the scope and significance of the study, research questions to be addressed and the perspective the study takes are briefly presented. An operational definition of CIP topic is provided and patterns of CIPT clauses are touched upon in a passing way. Chapter 2 presents previous research conducted on clause topics and topic structures. Attention is focused on views that provide the theoretical background against which my own study is made. Chapter 3 is a description of methodology. Data collection, creation of corpora and coding of data are illustrated there. Chapters 4 to 6 form the core of this study, as they explore CIP topics at different levels. In Chapter 4, units in their capacity as CIP topics are approached categorically and distributions of the categories in the corpus data are examined. Prototypical linguistic forms used as CIP topics are demonstrated and their features analyzed. Chapter 5 examines the syntactic environment of CIP topics—the syntactic patterns of CIPT clauses. Distributions of different types are explored and prototypical patterns are identified. A comparison is made between the prototypical pattern TSV in Chinese and the topicalization pattern OSV in English. Further, a parallel study based on data collected from two Chinese drama texts is carried out and an analysis of the English translations of CIPT clauses is made. In chapter 6, CIP topics are examined at a macro level—discourse level—from the angle of communicative function. Discoursal associations of CIP topics are probed into and the association patterns are identified. Cognitive features exhibited in the associations are discussed. Chapter 7 brings the study to a conclusion by summarizing the findings obtained, pointing out limitations of the study and presenting an outlook on future investigations.

Chapter 2　Literature review

Scholars give different interpretations of the term "topic" from different points of view. From the angle of syntax, topic as one constituent of a clause is the 'perspective' from which a clause, or sentence in Brown and Miller (1980: 360) and others, is viewed and what the clause is about. What is stated about the topic in a clause is the comment. Topic in this sense often corresponds with 'given' information. From the angle of discourse, Keenan and Schieffelin (1976) believe that topic is not a simple NP but a proposition (about which some claim is made or elicited). To the mind of Brown and Yule (1983:74), there will always be a set of possible expressions of the topic for any fragment of discourse. What is required is a characterization of 'topic' that would allow each of the possible expressions, including titles, to be considered (partially) correct. The factors of the context which are demonstrated in the text and which are necessary for an interpretation of the text form the contextual framework, i. e. the topic framework. The topic is entirely constituted within the framework. Factors contributing to the establishment of such a framework have little to do with discoursal associations investigated in this study and are hence beyond my concern. The following review of previous studies will focus primarily on thoughts that help to put in good form the ideas stuck to in the process of carrying out the current research.

2.1　Clause topics

2.1.1　Different understandings of topic

When delving into clause construction, Hockett (1958/1986) argues that while clauses can be described in terms of subject-predicate, they can also be described in terms of topic-comment. In English and other European languages, the topic often coincides with the subject whereas the comment with the predicate (Hockett 1958/1986:251). Consider the following examples used by this scholar:

(1) John run away.

(2) That new book by Thomas Guernsey I haven't read yet. (ibid)

In (1), "John" is both subject and topic and "run away" is predicate and comment. On the other hand, in (2), the constituent "That new book by Thomas Guernsey" plays the role of clause topic and "I haven't read yet" the comment. The personal pronoun "I" is the subject. He contends that topics in Chinese are quite different, though.

(3) 我今天城里有事。(ibid:253)

In example (3), "我" is the topic and "今天城里有事" is the comment. The constituent "今天城里有事" can stand alone if "我" is omitted. In this case, "今天" becomes the topic and "城里有事" the comment. Further, if "今天" is omitted, the remaining fragment "城里有事" can still stand as a clause in which "城里" is the topic and "有事" is the comment. Instance (3) can thus be considered a case of layered embedding in which three topic-comment structures are identified on different layers or levels. Such analysis, though confined to formal description and leaving the essence of topics unexplored, provides a starting point for studies of topics in Chinese.

According to Chao (1968/1979:45), subject is not obligatorily the agent of an act in a Chinese clause. Chao thus inclines to treat subject as topic since subject and predicate in some Chinese clauses are so loosely related that they will probably be perceived as ungrammatical in other languages. Consider his much reproduced instance below:

(4) 那回大火,幸亏消防队到得早。(ibid:60)

The noun phrase "那回大火" bears a very loose relationship with, or to be specific, has no selectional relation with the verb "到". For Chao, "那回大火" is better to be interpreted as a "topic" that sets a temporal framework for the clause. Although Chao's pioneering thought touches little upon the syntactic features and categorization of topics, it paves the way for subsequent investigations in the regard.

14

For Shi (2000), example (4) in which the noun phrase "那场火" can be considered as a dangling topic allows two interpretations as follows:

    (5) Na-chang huo xingkui xiaofang-dui lai-de-kuai, buran jiu hui shao-si bu-shao ren.
    'As for that fire, fortunately the fire brigade came quickly, otherwise (it) would have killed many people.'
    (6) Na-chang huo xingkui xiaofang-dui lai-de-kuai, buran na-ci women dou hui shao-si.
    'As for that fire, fortunately the fire brigade came quickly, otherwise we would all have been burnt to death at that time.'

The morpheme "xingkui" is treated as a connective adverb, forming part of the pairing phrase "xingkui… buran". It introduces an adverbial clause of cause. The second part of the phrase "buran" brings in the main clause of effect or would-be effect. In example (5), the clause initial noun phrase "na-chang huo" is related to the subject position in the main clause and becomes the antecedent of the zero form in that position. In (6), "na-chang huo" serves as the temporal adverbial of the main clause and is represented in the main clause by the demonstrative "na-ci". In either interpretation, the topic "na-chang huo" is related to a position inside the comment.

    Lu (1986: 81-83) opposes the idea of equating topic to subject. In his opinion, a subject in Chinese is not necessarily a topic. Conversely, what functions as a topic in Chinese is not necessarily a subject. The instances below are evidence that Lu gives:

    (7) a. 他不想参加。a' 这就是他不想参加的原因。(ibid)
       b. 至于水泥另外再想办法。(ibid)

It is not difficult to treat the personal pronoun "他" in (7a) as both subject and topic. On the other hand, there is no way to analyze "他" in (7a') as the topic of the clause though it is the subject of the embedded relative clause. In (7b), however, the clause initial prepositional phrase "至于水泥" can by no means be treated as the subject. The preposition "至于" is used simply to introduce the topic "水泥".

Fan and Hu（1992）contend that linguistic analysis involves three aspects: syntax, semantics and pragmatics. All of these aspects ought to be taken into account when a constituent is interpreted. Subject is a syntactic phenomenon while agent is a semantic one. Topic is pragmatically motivated. This idea is echoed in Gao（2004: 133-134）. In their famous typological study of language differences, Li and Thompson（1976）make it clear that "the evidence we have gathered from certain languages suggests that in these languages the basic constructions manifest a topic-comment relation rather than a subject-predicate relation". They believe that topic-comment sentences in topic-prominent languages are not derived but basic since, in these languages, "the basic structure of sentences favors a description in which the grammatical relation topic-comment plays a major role". Following their line of thought and going further, Xu and Liu（1998: 37）propose that a more innovative view should put us in the awareness that there are four basic clause elements in topic-prominent languages: V, S, O and T. Movement is not involved in the configuration of topic structures. A topic can co-exist with other elements and is thus unmarked. A clause in Chinese may contain both topic and subject, or either of them, or even neither of them（ibid: 57）. Consider the instances below from Xu and Liu（ibid）:

(8) a. 小张啊，他不来了。
    b. 小张啊，[ ]不来了。
    c. [ ]，他不来了。
    d. [ ]，[ ]不来了。

Both topic and subject occur in (8a) with the topic "小张" being designated by the particle "啊" and a succeeding prosodic pause. While instance (8b) contains only the topic "小张", (8c) contains only the subject "他". In (8d), both topic and subject are elliptical. Obviously the occurrence of topic is not compulsory.

Though scholars are not unanimous in interpreting topic, syntactic description of clauses in Chinese by means of topic-comment format has yet become convincing and necessary especially when subject-predicate format is not feasible.

2.1.2 Major syntactic properties of topics

Many researchers have touched upon properties of topics from the syntactic perspective. Detailed discussions are made mainly in Li and Thompson (1976), Xu and Langendoen (1985), and Shi (2000). While Xu and Langendoen will be referred to in section 2.1.3 where categorization of topics is presented and in section 2.2 where topic structures are dealt with, here I will concentrate on the idea put forward by Li and Thompson.

According to Li and Thompson, there are four basic types of languages: i) subject-prominent languages; ii) topic-prominent languages; iii) both subject-prominent and topic-prominent languages; iv) neither subject-prominent nor topic-prominent languages. English is a subject-prominent language whereas Chinese is a topic-prominent one. For a subject-prominent language, it is more appropriate to be described by taking 'subject' as basic. For a topic-prominent language, it is better to be described by taking 'topic' as basic. To achieve a clear understanding of the differences between subject-prominent and topic-prominent languages, characterizing topics syntactically is necessary. Li and Thompson argue that, on top of their difference in reference, say, topics are definite but subjects need not be so, topics differ from subjects in other aspects as well.

i. Selectional relations

The topic does not necessarily have a selectional relation with any verb in a sentence. This has already been evidenced by instance (4) mentioned above. Another example Li and Thompson provide is as follows:

(9) Nei-xie shumu shu-shen da.
　　'Those trees, the trunks are big.'

The topic "Nei-xie shumu" holds a whole-part relationship with the noun phrase "shu-shen", which is both a logical and syntactic subject of the predicate "大" in the comment. "Nei-xie shumu" is by no means related to the predicate though.

ii. Verb determines 'subject' but not 'topic'

This point is congruent with the previous one and can be seen as its continuation. The idea is easy to understand if we acknowledge that the topic is

17

what a speaker attempts to direct a hearer's attention to (Xu and Liu 1998:31). It means that when the topic sets the domain for a clause, it can be grammatically independent of the verb in the comment as shown in example (4) or independent of the predicate as in (9). In neither case is the topic affected by the predicate verb.

iii. Functional role

The functional role of the topic needs to be discussed in comparison with that of the subject. The functional role of the subject is twofold. First, a subject does not play any semantic role if it is an 'empty' or 'dummy' one. Second, if the subject is not empty, it can be defined within the syntactic boundaries of a sentence, or "characterized as providing the orientation or the point of view of the action, experience, state, etc., denoted by the verb" (Noonan, cited from Li and Thompson 1976). This is, as Li and Thompson claims, not true with the topic. As the center of attention, the topic sets a spatial, temporal, or individual framework within which the main predication holds. It does not have to be an argument of the verb. Although such a syntactic property together with properties listed in i) and ii) have much explanatory power for most topics in Chinese, they are invalidated to a great extent when analyses, say, made by Shi, prove that even a Chinese-style topic, a very dangling one, could be related to a position inside the comment.

The above properties unveiled by Li and Thompson do not apply in the present study since all the topics explored here exclusively bind an empty post-verbal position in the comment and thus play the semantic role of patient argument of the relevant verb.

iv. Verb agreement

In many languages, the verb obligatorily agrees with some grammatical property of the subject in a clause, but does not have to do so with that of the topic. The reason for this lies in the fact that a topic is often independent of the predicate in the comment while a subject is not. Such a difference between topic and subject does not explain much of Chinese because verbs in Chinese do not have morphological changes anyway even when the grammatical relation of subject-predicate is found.

v. Sentence initial position

While believing that the subject does not have to occur in sentence initial

18

position, Li and Thompson strongly hold that the topic always occupies that position. Further, in some languages like Lisu, Japanese, and Korean, the use of morpheme markers codifying the topic is mandatory. In other languages, like Lahu, the use of such morpheme markers is optional. This point is echoed in Tsao (1977/1995:37-39) with some revision. For this scholar, the topic, as far as Chinese is concerned, occupies the initial position of the first sentence in a topic chain rather than the initial position of a topic structure. As for the use of morpheme markers, he complements Li and Thompson's idea by stating that such particles as "啊", "呀", "呢", "嘛" and "吧" as well as prosodic pause can serve to separate the topic from the remainder of a topic structure. Nonetheless, Xu and Langendoen (1985) and Xu and Liu (1998) bring challenge to the claim about the topic's initial position either in a topic structure or in a topic chain. They contend that a topic structure may contain two topics (Xu and Langendoen 1985) or more topics (Xu and Liu 1998:51). The idea is expressed in formula (10a) and instantiated by (10b):

(10) a. TOP_1, TOP_2... TOP_n, X (Xu and Liu 1998:51)
    b. 小张,这件事,我认为[ ]办不了[ ]。(ibid:61)

In (10a), TOP_1, TOP_2 and TOP_n are all identified as main topics as long as they precede any non-topical element although only TOP_1 occupies the initial position. In (10b), both "小张" and "这件事" are analyzed as the main topics, respectively binding the preverbal and post-verbal gaps of the two-place verb "办" in the embedded clause. There are two other kinds of topics in addition to the main topics: subtopics and sub-subtopics. A subtopic occupies a post-subject position while a sub-subtopic occupies a post-verbal position either in a serial verb construction or in a double-object one. The instances below are cited from Xu and Liu:

(11) a. 我烈性酒从来不喝。(Xu and Liu 1998:61)
    b. 我请小张麽,负责业务工作,小李麽,负责行政工作。(ibid:76)
    c. 伊拨仔儿子末一幢房子,拨仔囝儿末一只钻戒。(ibid:77)

The noun phrase "烈性酒" in (11a) is a subtopic. Instance (11b) contains a serial

19

verb construction. The parallel noun phrases "小张" and "小李", both governed by the predicate verb "请", function as sub-subtopics marked by the particle "麼". They respectively play the semantic role of agent of the verb "负责". In (11c), the two indirect objects "儿子" and "囡儿", marked by the particle "末", also function as sub-subtopics. According to Xu and Liu, cases like (11b) and (11c) are very common in Shanghai dialect, in which topic-prominent phenomena are more diverse and frequent than in Mandarin Chinese.

As far as topic marker is concerned, the linguistic forms that serve this function, either lexical or grammatical, or even a combination of both, identified by Yuan (2003) are far more diverse than the forms identified by Tsao. My own exploration in this regard underpins Yuan's observation and will be presented later in detail in Chapter 5.

vi. Grammatical processes

The topic, unlike the subject, is not involved in such grammatical processes as reflexivization, passivization, Equi-NP deletion, verb serialization and imperativization since it is syntactically independent of the comment. However, this viewpoint meets challenge again. Tsao (1977/1995:39) holds that when the topic is also the subject, it may play a role in all such processes. For Yuan (1996), the 'topicalized subject', i.e. the topic, exerts similar influences as the basic subject, i.e. the grammatical subject, does in grammatical processes. Consider the clauses below cited from Yuan:

(12) a. 这种人$_i$我想[e$_i$]不会太亏待自己$_i$的
　　 b. 湿衣服你早一点挂出去晒晒
　　 c. 头发呢,他早被人剃光了　　　c'. 他呢,头发早被人剃光了
　　 d. [你]上我家吃早饭吧!　　　　d'. [早饭]你上我家吃吧!

It is obvious that the topics in (12a) ～ (12d) are all involved in one type of grammatical process or another. In (12a), the topic "这种人" governs the reflexivization through the gap. In (12b), the topic "湿衣服" governs the Equi-NP deletion in the serial verb construction. Instances (12c) and (12c') show that a topicalized element can be involved in passivization. In (12d) and (12d'), topics are involved in the process of imperitivization.

2.1.3 Categorization of topics

Not much works has been devoted to the categorization of topics although the literature on topics abounds in discussion about their syntactic properties. Topic classification varies when the focus of examination varies. Taking a syntactic stance, Xu and Langendoen (1985) identify six major categories of constituents that can function as topics. Taking a semantic stance, Xu and Liu (1998) identify four different types of topics depending on the semantic relations holding between topic and comment or an element or position in the comment. The four types can be further subclassified. These two ways of topic classification are briefly outlined in the following space.

Xu and Langendoen (1985) assume that six major categories of constituents can be topicalized in Chinese: NP (including quantifier phrases as a special case), S, S', VP, PrepP (prepositional phrase) and Postp (postpositional phrase). Each underlined part in the instances below exemplifies one syntactic category that can appear in TOP (ibid):

 (13) *Zhexie hua wo bu xiangxin.*
   'These words, I don't believe.'
 (14) *Ta hui shuo zhexie hua wo bu xiangxin.*
   'That he could have said these words, I don't believe.'
 (15) *Zhexie hua ta hui shuo wo bu xiangxin.*
   'That these words he could have said, I don't believe.'
 (16) *Zai zhuozi shang ta fang le jiben shu.*
   'On the table, he put some books.'
 (17) *Zhuozi shang you shu; chuang shang bu hui you shu.*
   'On the table there are some books; on the bed there cannot be any books.'
 (18) *Shuo zhexie hua wo bu xiangxin.*
   'Saying these words, I don't believe.'

The topicalized units in examples (13)~(18) are respectively NP, S, S', VP, PrepP and Postp. Clearly, a topicalized constituent itself can be a topic structure as shown in (15). In this case, the topicalized noun phrase *"Zhexie hua"* binds

21

the post-verbal gap in the embedded clause and is governed by the verb "*shuo*". Insightful as it is, such categorization is not flawless. The problem with distinguishing S from S' is pointed out earlier in Chapter 1. As far as NP in TOP is concerned, simply identifying its phrasal category is not telling enough. The reason is that such a topicalized item could bind different positions in the comment and thus deserves separate discussions. Phrasal exploration yet leaves this semantic aspect completely covered. The trouble is seen even in the scholars' own study. Consider (ibid):

    (19) 1968 *nian 8 yue 22 ri nei tian wo zhenghao* 21 *sui*.
       '(On) August 22, 1968, I was exactly 21 years old that day. '
    (20) 1968 nian 8 yue 22 ri wo yongyuan bu hui wangji.
       'August 22, 1968, I will never forget. '

In (19), the topicalized NP "1968 *nian 8 yue 22 ri*" binds the co-indexed adverbial element "*nei tian*" in the comment. The phrase sets the temporal framework within which the main predication holds. By contrast, in (20), the same NP is governed by the predicate verb "wangji". It binds the gap in the direct object position or patient argument position and represents a participant engaged in the activity described by the verb "wangji". The difference between the two noun phrases, however, fails to be captured when they are both treated as NP topics.

    As for the morpheme "*shang*" contained in the PostP appearing in TOP in (17), its interpretation has always been inconsistent. Some treat it as a locative noun (Wu and Cheng 1981:214; Zhang 1982:12; Hu 1995:285). Some treat it as a locative particle (Zhu 1982:44; Lv 1999:471; Liu 2002:140). No matter how it is interpreted, the fact is that the phrase "*zhuozi shang/chuang shang*" in (17) does not differ from the phrase "*zai zhuozi shang*" in (16) in essence in that, functionally, both of them serve to set a spatial domain for the clause. The preposition "*zai*" in (16) can be dropped without altering the meaning of the clause. Conversely, "*zai*" can be added before the phrase "*zhuozi shang/chuang shang*" in (17) without altering the meaning of the clause, either. In this sense, the significance of identifying post-prepositional phrase and pre-prepositional phrase as separate categories is definitely open to question.

To overcome such weaknesses, Xu and Liu (1998) take semantic factors into account and reclassify topics into such four types as argument and quasi-logical argument co-referring topics, domain topics, copy topics and clause topics. According to this reclassification, CIP topics explored in this study fall under the type of argument co-referring topics. While drawing on the sound insights achieved in these two categorizations, I try to further the exploration of CIP topics with both syntactic and semantic factors being taken into consideration at the level of syntactic research. More importantly, distribution of CIP topic categories will be investigated through frequency description. This certainly is necessary but has been neglected in the past since approaching topics from one single stance, either syntactic or semantic, confines such an attempt.

2.2 Topic structures

Topic structures are sometimes considered as containing, in addition to topic, a clause that functions as the comment. Xu and Langendoen (1985) argue that "the comment clause in a topic structure can be of any type: declarative, interrogative, imperative or exclamatory". Examples (19) and (20) above are typical cases in which the comment takes the form of a declarative. Comments of other clause types, like interrogative, imperative and exclamatory, are shown by these scholars as follows:

(21) *Zheben shu ni du guo ma?*
     'This book, have you read?'
(22) *Zhexie dongxi bie dong*!
     'These things, don't move!'
(23) *Zhezhang hua wo zhen xihuan*!
     'This picture, I really like!'

Similar assumption that a comment is realized as a clause is found in Shi (2000) when he proposes that

... a topic is an unmarked NP (or its equivalent) that precedes a clause and is related to a position inside the clause... namely, topic is what the current

23

sentence is set up to add new information to. The clause related to the topic in such a way is the comment.

The idea of equating a comment with a clause is dubious in two respects, though. First, logically speaking, clauses code propositions. The propositional content remains the same whether a clause is declarative, interrogative imperative or exclamatory. This makes it insignificant to distinguish comments according to their different syntactic forms. Second, although researchers try hard to distinguish 'subject' and 'topic', there are cases in which the two coincide. The comment hence does not take any clause form. The instance below cited from Brown and Miller (1980:330) is an illustration:

(24) a. John (G, L, T) took the largest kitten
     b. The largest kitten (G, T) was taken by John (L)
     c. The largest kitten (T), we (G, L) gave away

In (24), G, L and T respectively indicate grammatical, logical and thematic or psychological subject (seen as topic in this study). The three converge on the proper noun "John" in (24a). The comment, realized as the constituent "took the largest kitten", takes no form of a clause. Similar phenomenon as shown in (25) is interpreted by Xu and Liu (1998:59) as syntactical ambiguity:

(25) 小张不来了。

According to these scholars, a constituent like "小张" that precedes a verb can be assumed to be the subject if it plays the prototypical subject role of agent or experiencer and is not indicated by a prosodic pause or topic marker. This, however, as they continue, does not mean that the constituent cannot be analysed as the topic in some special contexts. Put simply, the noun phrase "小张" can be either the subject or topic of the clause. Such observations indirectly contradict and undermine the assumption that the comment takes the form of a clause in the way of a declarative, interrogative, imperative or exclamatory. In other words, a comment does not have to be a clause in form. Methodologically, this inference provides strong basis for my treatment of clauses like "两本书是同时写的" and

24

"这个木料原来是谁订的货呀", discussed previously in chapter 1, as CIPT clauses in which the initial NPs are analyzed as both the subject and topic.

2.3　Discourse functions of topics

Functionalists never interpret syntax as separate from discourse. According to Givon (1993a:25-26), only a small fraction of sub-components of syntax is used primarily to code the propositional information associated with a clause, and the bulk of sub-components of syntax is used primarily to code the discourse-pragmatics or communicative function of the clause. Downing (1995:9) states that word order variation conveys not only propositional information but also the need of the speaker or writer to establish a social or affective stance, to create text-level structures from sentence-level resources and to communicate in a way that is optimally matched to the text receiver's cognitive capacities. These views well explain why clause topics, as syntactic constituents, have been extensively described as pragmatically motivated.

Linguists of the Prague School like Danes and Enkvist observe in the 1970's that the theme, i. e. topic in this study, of a clasue functions as a cohesive device in a text. They describe such discourse feature as "thematic progression" and "theme dynamics" respectively (cf. Kurzon 1988). Li and Thompson (1976) hold that the topic is discourse-dependent and is best understood with respect to the discourse and extra-sentential considerations. Some Chinese scholars like Fan and Hu (1992), Yuan (1996), Shi (2000) and Gao (2004:134) make similar claims but yet do not further their points. It is primarily in Tsao that discourse functions of topics in Chinese are examined indepthly and systematically. Tsao (1977/1995:92-96) establishes that there are two ways for a topic to be connected with the previous discourse: one is *relating*, as exemplified in (26) below, and the other is *introductory*, as exemplified in (27):

(26) T：那：//这边的就是要卖掉？

　　C：这边因为里面旧旧脏脏，他说想油漆以后再卖。（Tsao 1977/1995:93）

(27) ······

　　T：对，月底搬家是吧？

　　C：啊，大概是。

T：新的地方离这里远不远？（ibid：95）

In (26)，the element "这边" serves as the topic in speaker T's utterance. In speaker C's utterance，"这边" is repeated and is again used as the topic. It ushers in the comment. The two utterances are therefore coherent. *"Relating"* of this kind is in fact semantic and tantamount to "lexical repetition" in Halliday and Hasan's (1976) terms. In (27)，the topicalized noun phrase "新的地方"，strictly speaking，is not given information since it has not been mentioned in the discourse prior to its occurrence. Yet thanks to its semantic relation with "搬家"，it represents some of the features expressed by "搬家" and can be regarded as a sub-topic and introducing a new aspect of the act denoted by the expression "搬家". Elements that hold semantic relations in the same way as "新的地方" does can be seen as，following Halliday and Hasan's analysis of lexical collocation，members of a lexical set. We defer detailed discussion of semantic relations holding between topics or items contained in topics and relevant constituents in contextual clauses until chapter 6 when the research is conducted on discoursal associations of CIP topics. Halliday and Hasan's cohesion theory will also be touched upon there.

The other aspect of discourse function that topics fulfill lies in the fact that they help to form "topic chain" (Tsao 1977/1995；Li and Thompson 1981). Below is another example from Tsao (1977/1995：98)：

(28) 那棵树花小，*a* ____叶子大，*b* ____很难看，所以 *c* ____我没有买。

For Tsao，the topicalized noun phrase "那棵树" in (28) co-refers with the gaps *a* ~ *c*，each of which stands for a zero form. There is no doubt that "那棵树" and "花小" form a topic-comment structure. By extension，"那棵树" forms topic-comment structures，too，with "叶子大"，"很难看" and "我没有买" respectively but in an indirect way. In this discourse chunk，"那棵树" controls the deletion of the topics in all the other clauses succeeding the first one. Consequently，the clauses in (28) constitute a topic chain and the noun phrase "那棵树" fulfils a chaining function. Similar phenomenon is noticed by Wu and Cheng (1981) but interpreted in a different way. Consider：

26

（29）他的文章，我读过了，____很有趣。（ibid：298）

In line with traditional grammar, Wu and Cheng consider "文章" the "patient-subject", which in this study, constitutes the head of the noun phrase in TOP. Where Wu and Cheng's understanding is on a parallel with Tsao's is that "文章" controls the deletion of the subject in the subsequent clause. Thus the clause initial zero form there refers back to the noun phrase "他的文章" and the two clauses are coherently connected.

There are cases where the coreferential zero form does not occupy the clause initial position. Consider：

（30）这个英文句子真难，我不懂a ____，他也不懂b ____。（Tsao 1977/1995：97）

In the above discourse chunk, the topic of the first clause "这个英文句子" is anaphorically referred to by the zero forms represented by a and b in the second and third clause. Or conversely, the item "这个英文句子" controls the deletion of the direct object in the succeeding two clauses. Still the clauses form a topic chain as a result of the chaining function fulfilled by the noun phrase "这个英文句子".

Some researchers examine semantic relations holding between topics and elements contained in contextual clauses from a similar angle while using different labels. Their arguments, like Tsao's argument, are vulnerable to criticism in two ways, though. First, since topics in all these studies are not categorized, descriptions of discourse functions of topics are apparently too general to accommodate a specific type of topics. Second, no quantitative means is employed to gauge and examine such discourse functions. This makes the descriptions vague, and the extent to which topics are related with relevant constituents in contextual clauses fails to be revealed.

In spite of the limitations, Tsao's pioneering assumption that Chinese is a discourse-oriented language is thought-provoking. His analyses of discourse functions performed by clause topics are constructive to the present study and serve both as a starting point and a guideline for the exploration of discoursal associations on the part of CIP topics though his study and mine are methodologically different. Where I go further is that both qualitative and quantitative investigations are made and that discourse functions of CIP topics are categorically focused on and empirically delved into.

Chapter 3   Methodology

In the attempt to investigate categories of CIP topics, types of CIPT clauses and discoursal associations on the part of CIP topics, two mini-sized corpora based on tokens collected from spontaneous spoken Mandarin Chinese are established in this study: one consisting of CIPT clauses and the other consisting of discourse chunks in which CIPT clauses are embedded. In fact, the former corpus is the basis of the latter while the latter is an extension of the former on discourse level. In the sections to follow, I will describe data collection, creation of the corpora, data coding and data processing.

3.1   Data

3.1.1   Data sources

The sources of data are television programs tape-recorded or video-recorded by myself over a period of approximately more than three years. The recorded programs are of interactive nature. They include dialogues, interviews, panel discussions, narrations and lectures on a variety of subjects but exclude talk shows. In all, thirty-three programs are obtained and are converted into electronic files that can be played on such audio-visual tools as Realplayer or Windows Media Player. The broadcast time and length of each program are labeled and its title and source written down (see Appendix Ⅱ). The sample programs add up to 1,052 minutes in length with each lasting for about 32 minutes on average. In the process of sample selection, factors such as age, educational background, register (formal / informal), speech style (planned / unplanned) and gender (male / female) are taken into account so that spoken Mandarin is sufficiently represented in the data and that individual speaker variation in the use of CIPT clauses will not skew the results. The data used in the study are drawn from the sample programs and are transcribed by myself. Accordingly, the conclusions reached based on those data are confined to the genre of spoken Mandarin.

3.1.2 Data collection and transcription

Data collection forms a demanding and time-consuming part of this study in the sense that spoken language is, compared to written language, often less formal and even ungrammatical. Ellipsis, speech repair, pause filler, recycling, absence of inter-utterance pause and overlap, all are normal occurrences in the samples and sometimes make it difficult to arrive at a firm and rigid decision, even when repeated listening is tried, about whether or not an utterance constitutes a felicitous clause or where the boundaries of an utterance lie. The data employed are of two types: CIPT clauses and discourse chunks that contain CIPT clauses. The gathering of CIPT clauses takes three steps. First, listen through a sample file and record the position where a CIPT utterance① occurs in a way that both the file number and the point at which the utterance begins is written down. Such a position code is a six-digit figure. The beginning two digits are the file number. The two digits in the middle indicate the minute from which a CIPT utterance begins while the last two digits indicate the second from which the utterance begins so as to provide an accurate recording of its occurrence in the file. Suppose the position of a CIPT clause is recorded as "120315", the utterance can be located at the temporal point of 3'15" in File No. 12. Second, search for the target CIPT utterance according to the position recorded and transcribe the utterance. Third, compare what has been transcribed—the CIPT clause—with the target utterance and check over until minor details like prosodic pause or insertion within the utterance are fully captured. To listen repeatedly to a target CIPT utterance is necessary when assurance is to be made about a transcription. When discourse chunks are to be gathered, transcribing involves strings of contextual utterances that respectively precede and succeed a target utterance such that the CIPT clause occupies the middle position in a discourse chunk. The steps taken to transcribe these stretches of utterances are: first, search for an identified CIPT utterance according to its position in the sample file and listen to

---

① A token is an utterance or a string of utterances in prosodic form in an electronic file before being transcribed. It is treated as a clause or a discourse chunk only after being transcribed, i.e., written down, in orthographic form.

the four contextual utterances occurring prior to it and transcribe them[①]; second, listen to the four contextual utterances succeeding the CIPT utterance and transcribe them; third, compare the transcriptions with the recording and check over. To avoid ambiguity in the identification of an utterance—either a CIPT utterance or a contextual utterance, a uniform criterion for transcribing is set as: if an utterance conveys a complete propostional meaning and prosodically forms a separate tone unit, it is taken as a felicitous clause whether it is of canonical word order or of non-canonical word order. An intra-utterance pause does not affect the identification of an utterance as a felicitous clause if the utterance conveys a complete propositional meaning. When transcribing contextual utterances of non-subject-predicate construction, I draw on views about clause types in Wu and Cheng (1981: 364), Wu (1985: 440-442) and Liu (2002: 254). One-word responding utterances like "是" or "对" and addressing utterances like "老师" or "孩子" are treated as felicitous contextual clauses. On the other hand, expressions such as "你说", "你看" or "你想" that mainly serve to attract the hearer's attention are treated as insertions but not felicitous contextual clauses.

The diverse lengths of inter-utterance pause pose further difficulties for transcribing: it is hard to punctuate transcriptions with certainty by means of a comma or a full stop or some other graphic symbols. In Thornborrow and Wareing's (2000:122) study, they comply with the transcription convention that "pauses less than half a second long are shown as a full stop". Brown and Yule (1983: 163) divide pauses into three types in their study of information structures: extended pauses (ranging from 3.2 ~ 16 seconds), long pauses (ranging from 1.0 ~ 1.9 seconds) and short pauses (ranging from 0.1 ~ 0.6 seconds). Since my attention is focused on identifying felicitous clauses rather than on marking pauses of different lengths with different punctuation marks like a comma or a full stop, I choose to adopt the slash symbol "/" in transcribing to demarcate utterance boundaries and ignore length difference in pause between utterances and syntactic difference among utterances such as declarative, imperative or interrogative. The symbol " ∨ " is used to mark an intra-utterance pause such that the prosodic feature is retained when an utterance is recorded.

---

① Though the limit of a discourse stretch preceding or succeeding a CIPT utterance is set on four contextual utterances, more than four contextual utterances might be transcribed when necessary.

3.2 Creation of the corpora

When data collection is completed and transcriptions are keyboarded, two corpora are respectively created in Microsoft word form: one for CIPT clauses and the other for discourse chunks. The former corpus contains 217 tokens, i. e. , 217 CIPT clauses (see Appendix I) of 3,170 words. It provides the basis for studies of both CIP topic categories and of CIPT clause types. The latter corpus also contains 217 tokens, yet in the form of discourse chunks. Each chunk comprises 9 clauses—1 CIPT clause and 8 contextual clauses. Put differently, a total of 1,953 clauses, including 217 CIPT clauses—roughly 33,590 words—are incorporated. Grounded on these two corpora, sub-corpora are further created for different purposes of the study at different stages.

3.3 Coding of data

Data are coded in different ways with the proceeding of the study. To achieve the goal of investigating categories of linguistic forms that function as CIP topics, the topics are classified and sub-classified and coded correspondingly. When exploring syntactic types of CIPT clauses, clause constructions are examined. The tokens are also classified and sub-classified and correspondingly coded. When discoursal associations of CIP topics are investigated, semantic connections between CIP topics or elements contained in them and elements in contextual clauses are coded and values signaling connections at different points are assigned. Evidently, the way of coding varies when the focus of study varies. So do the codes adopted in order to achieve different goals set at different stages. When coding is finished, codes are keyboarded. Different sets of codes, represented by letters or numbers or both, are arranged in different columns for different variables. Eventually, data are designated both symbolically and numerically so that they are suitable for Microsoft Excel system to understand and process and that a token can be retrieved for specific examination at a certain point of time. Moreover, discoursal association patterns can be investigated on the basis of CIP topic categorization or of CIPT clause classification. Details of coding will be specified respectively in relevant chapters to follow.

3.4 Data processing

When all the codes are keyboarded, Word files are converted into Excel files. Excel 2003 is used to carry out statistical analysis. Not as powerful as statistical packages such as SAS or SPSS, though, the tool adequately serves the purpose of the present study.

Chapter 4   Linguistic units
as CIP topics

4.1 Introduction

This chapter sets out to investigate categories of linguistic units that function as CIP topics and their distributions in the corpus data. The chapter is organized as: section 4.2 presents research questions; section 4.3 explains how the data are coded and sub-coded for automatic processing and for categorical analysis; section 4.4 reports and discusses the results; section 4.5 compares phrasal categories of units in TOP in Chinese with those in English; lastly, section 4.6 presents a summary of the chapter.

4.2 Research questions

The questions that this chapter aims to address include:
1) What categories and subcategories of linguistic units can fulfill the role of CIP topic and how do they distribute in the corpus data?
2) How do prototypical categories and subcategories of such units differ from non-prototypical ones?
3) In what way do phrasal categories of units in TOP identified in Chinese differ from those in English?

4.3 Data coding

Data coding goes hand in hand with classifying and sub-classifying the linguistic units that function as CIP topics. The task is primarily a qualitative one. When a constituent that plays the role of CIP topic is a noun phrase, the code "NP" will be assigned. If the constituent is a verb phrase or an embedded clause, the code "VP" or "EC" will be assigned. When all the tokens are coded and automatically categorized by Excel 2003, six categories are identified: NP, VP, EC, CP (classifier phrase), DEM (demonstrative) and AP (apposition construction). Within each of these categories, the members are not always in the uniform linguistic form. This makes sub-coding of the corpus data necessary, which is, in effect, a process of subcategorinzing data. When a constituent is sub-coded, the code it is assigned contains information about both its category and subcategory. The information about the category of a topicalized constituent is provided by letters in upper case. The information about the subcategory of a topicalized constituent is given by letters in lower case. For instance, a code like "NPdet" means that the topicalized item it stands for is a noun phrase containing a demonstrative determiner. The code can thus be represented as determiner $\in$ NP. The sign "$\in$", borrowed from set theory, denotes the relationship of "belong to". Here the demonstrative determiner "这" is viewed as an element of the NP which corresponds to a set. A topicalized constituent like "这条鱼"[1] in the CIPT clause "这条鱼他很难拉到岸上来" is a case where the code "NPdet" applies. If two or more pieces of information are written down for elements contained in a constituent in TOP, they are parallelly designated by means of the symbol "+". Further detailed information about such elements is provided by subcripts. A code like "APvp+np$_{det}$" means that the topicalized constituent is an apposition construction that consists of a verb phrase appositive and a noun phrase one. The noun phrase in turn contains a demonstrative determiner. The CIP topic "装错房子这样的事情" in the topic structure "装错房子这样的事情是可以避免的" instantiates such a code. The code is explained as verb phrase $\subset$ AP, noun phrase $\subset$ AP and determiner $\in$ NP. The sign "$\subset$" denotes the relationship of "be included in". Here the appositives—the verb phrase "装错房子" and the noun phrase "这样的事情"—are viewed as two separate subsets of equal syntactic status within the apposition construction "装错房子这样的事情", which corresponds to a set. This is so even when one of the appositives comprises only one element. For instance, the code "APpron+np$_{det+mod}$", standing for the topic "它这个山水画" in the CIPT clause "它这个山水画是后人临的也好", indicates that the topicalized apposition construction comprises a pronoun "它"

---

① Since classifiers like "条" and "件" etc. cannot stand alone without accompanying a determiner or number, they are not singled out and marked in the process of coding.

and a co-referring noun phrase "这个山水画". Both appositives are considered subsets though the pronoun can not be further segmented while the noun phrase "这个山水画" can be analyzed as consisting of the determiner "这个", the modifier "山水" and the head noun "画". For a token that cannot be subcategorized，the code and sub-code it is assigned coincide and are represented in upper case only. Table 4.1 is an illustration of all the categories and sub-categories of CIP topics identified in the corpus data and the codes and sub-codes they are assigned correspondingly.

Table 4.1　Categories and sub-categories of CIP topics

Types	Codes	Sub-codes	Examples from the corpus data
I	NP (Noun phrase)	1. NPpos (possessive∈NP)	他的机会也不会给你了/ 秦可卿的丧事都办完了/
		2. NPbare (NP = bare noun)	房子我们住着/
		3. NPmod (modifier∈NP)	眼前的事情就算是处理完了/ 其他东西他们一般就不展出了/
		4. NPdet (determiner∈NP)	这条鱼他很难拉到岸上来/
		5. NPuni-q (universal quantifier∈NP)	所有的"长"我都不做的/
		6. NPex-q (existential quantifier∈NP)	有的话他也好像还不太明白/
		7. NPcp (classifier phrase⊂NP)	两个底版一重叠/
		8. NPg-q (generic quantifier⊂NP)	连一个中学毕业证书都没有/
		9. NP*de* (NP = *de* structure)	剩下的也没用在家里/
		10. NPind + g-q (indefinite pronoun∈NP, generic quantifier⊂NP)	你就觉得某一步棋你要看见了/
		11. NPprop (NP = proper noun)	张爱玲他们根本不承认/
II	CP (Classifier phrase)	1. CPdet + num (determiner∈CP, number∈CP)	那九个我们就带走了/

(Continued)

Types	Codes	Sub-codes	Examples from the corpus data
II	CP (Classifier phrase)	2. CPdet (determiner∈CP)	这点写错了呀/
		3. CPnum (number∈CP)	她诈骗来的钱一部分拿去办出国手续了/
III	DEM (Demonstrative)	DEM	这我也不知道/ 这些如果都知道/ 那个专家不会翻/
IV	VP (Verb phrase)	VPdet (determiner∈VP)	出这种事开发商也实在是想不到/
V	EC (Embedded clause)	1. EC	她下放我并不知道/
		2. ECdet (determiner∈EC)	这纸什么时候捅破的也不知道/
VI	AP (Apposition)	1. APpron + np$_{det + mod}$ (pronoun⊂AP, noun⊂AP, determiner∈np, modifier∈np)	它这个山水画是后人临的也好/
		2. APcit$_{[mod]}$① + np$_{det}$ (citation⊂AP, np⊂AP, mod∈citation, determiner∈np); [zheige +]② APcit + np$_{cp}$ (citation⊂AP, np⊂AP, classifier phrase∈np)	"仁义礼智"的"仁"这个概念一提出来/ 这个"逗漏"两个字啊希望你注意/
		3. APvp + np$_{det}$ (verb phrase⊂AP, noun phrase⊂AP, determiner∈np)	装错房子这样的事情完全是可以避免的/
		4. APec + np$_{det}$ (embedded clause⊂AP, noun phrase⊂AP, determiner∈np)	钥匙能互开这样的事并没有签入合同/
		5. APnp$_1$ + np$_{2[det]}$ (noun phrase$_1$⊂AP, noun phrase$_2$⊂AP, determiner∈np$_2$)	连云港老家我们都去了/ 养老院这个制度能不能推行开/

① The square brackets indicate that the elements enclosed are unstressed and/or can be omitted without altering the meaning of a clause.

② The morpheme "zheige" in this case is considered a topic marker. Such a treatment will be discussed in detail in chapter 5.

36

The codes listed in the second column of Table 4.1 represent the categories of linguistic units identified as appearing in TOP. The sub-codes represent the subcategories of units in TOP. Beneath most of the sub-codes, one or more than one expressions, enclosed in round brackets, are given that explain the construction of a CIP topic a sub-code represents. In box AP-2, two sub-codes are put together rather than separated. This is because if the elements in square brackets are dropped from the sub-code in either case, the topicalized constituents they indicate do not differ dramatically and can still be considered subsuming under the same subcategory.

For the purpose of distributional investigation of the categories and subcategories, both categorical and subcategorical codes need to be processed and analyzed. This is why the data are arranged in a format in which each token bears, in addition to the positional code it has already borne, codes of these two kinds—one telling the category, the other telling the subcategory. Table 4.2 gives a sample of the format.

Table 4.2　Sample data coded for automatic processing

	Categories	Subcategories	Examples from the corpus data	Position
1.	DEM	DEM	那个是在开始时候没有想到的／	022946
2.	CP	CPdet + num	那九个我们就带走了／	050726
3.	NP	NPpos	他的机会也不会给你了／	050755
4.	NP	NPmod	其他东西他们一般就不展出了／	060140
5.	AP	APpron + np$_{det + mod}$	它这个山水画是后人临的也好／	061015
6.	NP	NPmod	后宫里头就顾及不到／	062510
7.	NP	NPdet	这首歌演唱得很有弹性／	071000
8.	NP	NPuni-q + mod	所有香港的比赛我都去参加／	070545
9.	NP	NPmod	麻将牌我不会／	080124
10.	NP	NPbare	长袍马褂儿穿着／	080530
11.	EC	ECdet	这纸什么时候捅破的也不知道／	080810

	Categories	Subcategories	Examples from the corpus data	Position
12.	VP	VP	怎么捅破的不知道/	080815
13.	NP	zheige + NPbare	这个服装为什么要改革呢/	090808
14.	NP	NPmod + det	历史上面已经存在的这种有地域特色的文化可能今天我们已经看不到了/	092700
15.	NP	NPmod + det	像横尸遍野ᵛ这个血流成河的这一种惨烈战争场面它几乎没有经历过/	111730
16.	DEM	DEM	这我们都知道/	131215
17.	AP	APvp + np$_{det}$	装错房子这样的事情完全是可以避免的/	162340
18.	NP	NPde	你对你父亲做的你觉得也是应该的/	200649
19.	AP	APmod + cit + np$_{det}$	后面的"共同参与ᵛ父亲所有遗产由大姑拥有ᵛ吕艳放弃继承"这些话ᵛ全部都是吕科华利用这些空格后加的/	201415
20.	AP	APvp + np$_{det}$	搬迁这事是在 2004 年底就已经确定了/	201800
21.	AP	APcit + np	《读书》杂志是很多老头办的/	210608

The occurrences of each category and subcategory are calculated by means of the "COUNTIF" function in Excel 2003. The distribution of the frequencies can subsequently be obtained.

4.4 Results and discussion

This section reports the results yielded relevant to the research question about the distributions of categories and subcategories of linguistic units playing the role of CIP topics in the corpus data. In addition, it attempts to reveal the features of the prototype category and subcategory as well as to give a complete rundown on the features of the non-prototype category and subcategory.

4.4.1 Categorical distribution of units as CIP topics

The distribution of the categories yielded through statistical analysis is represented in Table 4.3 below:

Table 4.3 Distribution of the 217 sample CIP topics

	Categories	N	%
1.	NP	158	72.8
2.	DEM	20	9.2
3.	EC	15	6.9
4.	AP	13	6.0
5.	CP	6	2.8
6.	VP	5	2.3
	Total	217	100.0

It is noted earlier that the six categories are, roughly speaking, paradigmatic alternatives. That is, the choice of one phrase category excludes the choice of other phrase categories. Understandably, different categories do not distribute evenly in the corpus. Strong restrictions govern the occurrences of some categories in TOP. The competition among the categories to appear in TOP as shown in Table 4.3 can be depicted in the following hierarchy of tendency:

$$NP > DEM > EC > AP > CP > VP$$

Figure 4.1 Access of categories to TOP

Figure 4.1 clearly demonstrates the uneven distributions of the categories identified. Such an order indicates that the categories' tendencies to play the role of CIP topic rank hierarchically from the strongest to the weakest: units of the NP category are the most frequent whereas units of the VP category are the most infrequent. Units of other categories lie in between the two. From the functional point of view, frequency and markedness are related. Markedness is a phenomenon largely relative to context. "The marked category is less frequent, while the unmarked is more frequent" (Givon 1995b:25). Following this line of thought, in the context of CIPT clauses that are marked structures themselves, distinction can be drawn between marked and unmarked constituents in TOP on the basis of the frequency criterion. Noun phrases, accounting for the overwhelming majority of the units in TOP, predominate in the corpus data and therefore form an unmarked category. Other phrases have no predominant status and form marked categories. Classifier phrases and verb phrases, in particular, form marginal categories due to their similarly low frequencies. The measurement of frequency also sheds light on prototypicality. The correlation among frequency, markedness and prototypicality is illustrated by "a study of the Rigvedic verb in which the 'prototypical' verb form, third-person singular present active indicative, occurred 1, 404 times, whereas a highly marked verb form, second-person dual mediopassive perfect optative, did not occur at all" (Greenberg, cited from Croft 2000:125-126). Obviously, the evidence for category markedness is essentially the same as the evidence for prototype category and the unmarked category is also the prototype category. The unmarked NP category thus becomes the prototype category in the present study.

Presumably the hierarchical distribution of the categories in question has much to do with the properties inherent in CIP topics and with the extent to which the features of a category overlap with those properties. Namely, the bigger the overlap is, the more a category fits the role, and the higher its frequency is. Although clause topic has not been defined to the satisfaction of all scholars to date, its key properties are not beyond agreement. First, according to Li and Thompson, a topic must be definite when reference is taken into account. Xu and Liu (1998:251) give a broader picture and argue that if an element has definite reference, codes generic or given or activated information, or denotes shared knowledge, it is then very apt to be topicalized. Second, from semantic point of view, a CIP topic ought to be the internal argument of a relevant verb in the comment and thus a participant involved in the state or event coded by that verb. This property gives pronominal forms the priority to be topicalized since they denote entities, either concrete or abstract, that often trigger the production of an information structure. Thirdly, the initial or near initial position favors simple, light or short morphosyntactic forms and expels complex or long ones. This squares with the principle of end-weight (Qrirk et al. 1985:1040) that operates at the level of structural complexity and allows the new information to be stated more fully than the given with a longer, heavier structure (ibid: 1361-1362). Syntactically, heavy, long or complex constituents should go after light, short or simple ones. Cognitively, such arrangement facilitates information processing. As a result, the chance for complex or long forms to appear in TOP is considerably reduced and the scope of pronominal forms eligible for the role of CIP topic is narrowed. All the above properties impose restrictions on some categories as well as subcategories that otherwise could become prototype categories or subcategories. The subsequent sections are aimed to delve into the features of each category or subcategory that license it to be or prevent it from being a prototype.

4.4.2　Noun phrases: the prototype category

Although NP category overwhelmingly predominates in the data, accounting for 72.8% of all CIP topics, members of its subcategories do not distribute evenly due to their differences in morphosyntactic form. According to their length, the noun phrases can be divided into two groups: simple noun phrases and complex noun phrases. Their distribution in the corpus data is given in Table 4.4 below:

Table 4.4　Distribution of simple and complex noun phrases as CIP topics

Length of noun phrases	Number	%
Simple noun phrases	137	63.1
Complex noun phrases	21	9.7
Total	158	72.8

$x^2 = 170.329$, $p = .000$

Chi-square test shows that there is a significant differnce between simple noun phrases and complex noun phrases in terms of their occurrences. The huge gap in frequency between them necessitates separate discussion and investigation of each group so that the features that fit a group for or prevent it from playing the role of CIP topic are dealt with in detail.

4.4.2.1　Simple noun phrases

Simple noun phrases are differentiated from complex ones on the grounds of their formal simplicity. In other words, they are brief and short in form, comprising components that can be divived once or twice. Specifically, when a simple noun phrase comprises only one component, it is either a bare noun (under which *de* construction is subsumed) or a proper noun. When a simple noun phrase comprises two or three elements, there are six lexical formations: ① noun phrase containing a demonstrative determiner and a head noun; ② noun phrase containing

41

a modifier—either marked by the particle de or not marked at all—and a head noun; ③ noun phrase containing a possessor as determiner and a head noun; ④ noun phrase containing a classifier phrase as modifier and a head noun; ⑤ noun phrase containing a universal quantifier and a head noun; ⑥ lastly, noun phrase embracing an existential quantifier and a head noun. Altogether, eight subcategories fall under simple noun phrases. They are instantiated as follows:

(1) NPprop   张爱玲
   NPbare（including NPde） 房子;其余的
   NPdet   这样的事,这件事
   NPmod   学生运动
   NPpos   他的机会
   NPcp   两个底版
   NPuni-q   所有的"长"
   NPex-q   有的话

Table 4.5 below presents the results of the investigation into the distribution of subcategories listed above.

Table 4. 5 Distribution of subcategories of simple noun phrases

	Subcategories	Number	%
1.	NPprop	6	2.8
2.	NPbare (including NP*de*)	32	14.8
3.	NPdet	45	20.7
4.	NPmod	38	17.5
5.	NPpos	6	2.8
6.	NPcp	3	1.4
7.	NPuni-q	6	2.8
8.	NPex-q	1	0.5
	Total	137	63.1

Three out of the eight subcategories strikingly stand out for their high frequencies:

NPdet (20.8%), NPmod (17.5%) and NPbare (14.8). By contrast, all the other five subcategories occur only occasionally or even rarely, showing very low frequencies: NPprop (2.8%), NPpos (2.8%), NPcp (1.4%), NPuni-q (2.8%), NPex-q (0.5%). Accordingly, the three frequent subcategories become prototypical whereas the other five non-prototypical or marginal. Different referring status is assumed to be a major cause of the disparity between prototypical and non-prototypical or marginal subcategories though their members may be equal in other aspects—being a patient argument and simple in form. The fact that noun phrases containing demonstrative determiner have the highest frequency shows that such units, expressing definite referential meaning, are most likely to be topicalized and can be viewed as typical forms of CIP topics. Modifiers contained in noun phrases provide specific details about the head nouns. They help increase the degree of definite reference expressed by those noun phrases. Such phrases also show very strong tendency to be topicalized and their frequency is only second to nominal expressions embracing a demonstrative determiner. As far as bare nouns are concerned, investigation of their discoursal associations reveals that such nouns have a strong tendency to be anaphorically cohesive. Consider the following:

(2) ……改变挺大的/但是细节我不想多说/
(3) A：……要惩罚一下这个小弟弟/取消他今后的遗产继承权/没想到这一商量发现了更大的问题/
    B：房子给了小儿子/

The topicalized bare noun "细节" in example (2) denotes activated information because it is presupposed by and semantically related to the nominal phrase "改变" in the preceding clause. In example (3), the bare noun "房子" in TOP in speaker B's turn is semantically related with the nominal phrase "遗产" that occurs in the previous discourse in speaker A's turn. It has two interpretations. First, given that the referent coded by "遗产" comprises several items, say, money, a house, a workshop, etc., the bare noun "房子" holds a part-of-whole relation with the nominal "遗产" and codes activated information. Second, if the referent coded by the nominal "遗产" comprises only one item, a house, "房子" then has a definite reference. In neither case is the bare noun used generically. This observation calls into question the claim that bare nouns or nominals preceded by a null determiner have a generic interpretation (Chen 1987; Radford 2002:152) or an existential interpretation (Radford 2002:152). Functionally, the anaphoric association or cohesiveness on the part of bare nouns presumably gives rise to their definite reference or coding of activated information and has much explanatory value in terms of their high frequency in the corpus data.

The non-prototypical or marginal units are subject to various constraints. Unique denotation is taken to be symptomatic of proper nouns. When such nouns, specifically personal names, are identified as playing the role of CIP topics, however, definite reference does not necessarily help increase their chance of occurring in TOP. Consider:

(4) a. 嘉当是超越不了/
   b. 张爱玲他们根本不承认/

The two topic structures are ambiguous in that each has different interpretations. The first interpretation of example (4a) is that someone, whose name is dropped, cannot surpass Cartan[①]. The second interpretation is that "Cartan" cannot surpass someone whose name is not mentioned. The first interpretation of example (4b) is that "他们" do not acknowledge (the fame of) "张爱玲". The second interpretation is that "张爱玲" and some other people as a whole do not acknowledge (someone else's fame) or they do not admit something. Only with reference to the contexts in which the structures are used, the first interpretation in both cases can be obtained. The reason for the ambiguity of the structures is that the initial elements—being human in nature—are more likely to be interpreted as the agent or one member of the mass agent that performs the act specified than to be interpreted as the patient affected by the act. It is so especially when the real agent does not occur as in (4a). Ambiguous interpretation has a restrictive effect on the use of personal names. Such names thus appear only occasionally in TOP. It is not certain whether human determiner is confined in a noun phrase fulfilling the role of CIP topic. Nonetheless, the fact that noun phrases containing a possessor as determiner occur very infrequently in TOP somewhat suggests such a correlation.

---

① Élie Joseph Cartan (1869—1951), French mathematician.

The definite reference of noun phrases embracing a classifier phrase is often context-dependent. Namely, the numeral used in the classifier phrase designates the items mentioned earlier such that the entire noun phrase takes on definite referential meaning. To illustrate this briefly, consider the following discourse chunk:

(5) 其实读《野火》的读者要把《孩子你慢慢来》那本书要并着看/为什么呢/两本书是同时写的/

The numeral "两" in the CIP topic "两本书" denotes the two book titles mentioned prior to the topic structure: "《野火》" and "《孩子你慢慢来》". The noun phrase "两本书" is thus used to refer definitely to these two books. On top of this, as far as the succeeding discourse is concerned, the item has the relating function of previewing (see detailed discussion in chapter 6). Subject to such use conditions, expressions containing a classifier phrase are rarely topicalized in the corpus data.

Turning to universal quantifier (symbolized as $\forall$) and existential quantifier (symbolized as $\exists$), they have a logical origin, touched upon mainly in the respect of quantified natural deduction. Semantically, the former has a generic interpretation and denotes universal quantification expressing "for all". The latter has a partitive interpretation expressing the concept of "some" or, more exactly, "there is at least one". Universal quantifiers in Chinese include such linguistic units as "每", "所有", "任何" and "一切" that precede a head noun. Interrogative expressions like "谁" and "什么" can be used as universal quantifiers in the same way. Adverbs like "都" or "也" usually occur when a universal quantifier is used. In Xu and Liu (1998: 193-202), universal quantifiers are very likely to be topicalized or even obligatorily to be topicalized when they are used for definite reference in the way that generic noun phrases are used. Partitive existential quantifiers, when following a definite or generic item, express anaphoric reference. They may also be used in coordinating clauses and express contrastiveness. In either case, they tend to appear in TOP. In the present study, both the topicalization of universal quantifier and that of existential quantifier have restrictive use conditions. Consider:

(6) 从 1975 年开始参加歌唱比赛/我是每年都参加/所有香港的比赛我都去

参加/

（7）<u>有的话</u>他也好像还不太明白/听不懂的/有一个老师说/你等着/我哪一天得上你们家去/小孩说/真的/老师/什么时候去/

In example（6），the underlined universal noun phrase "所有香港的比赛" in TOP relates to the item "歌唱比赛" in the preceding discourse in a way that the formerly occurring item has to hold a part-of-whole relation with the expression in TOP. The configuration of such a semantic relation requires that the item denoting the part go ahead of and usher in the universal noun phrase denoting the whole. The latter builds upon what is said previously or what is already known to both the speaker and the hearer. In（7），the existential noun phrase in TOP "有的话" has an indefinite reference. It functions as a prelude to the subsequent discourse and is specified by the direct speech. Such a semantic relation can be analyzed as generalisation-example（cf. Hoey 1983：134-138）. Coherence is thus achieved in the chunk. Much confined by discourse factors，universal noun phrase in TOP is quite infrequent while existential noun phrase is rare occurring only once in the corpus.

4. 4. 2. 2 Complex noun phrases

Compared to simple noun phrases，complex noun phrases are long in form，comprising components that can be divided three or more times. In all，eight subcategories subsume under this group. Their lexical formations are：① noun phrase containing one or two modifiers, a demonstrative determiner and a head noun（the order of the components preceding the head noun may not be fixed）；② noun phrase containing a possessor as determiner，a modifier and a head noun；③ noun phrase containing a possessor as determiner，a demonstrative determiner，a modifier and a head noun；④ noun phrase containing an optional modifier，a demonstrative determiner，a classifier phrase and a head noun；⑤ noun phrase containing a classifier phrase，a modifier and a head noun（the order of the classifier phrase and modifier preceding the head noun is not fixed）；⑥ noun phrase containing a modifier，a generic quantifier and a head noun；⑦ noun phrase containing a possessor as determiner，a modifier，a universal quantifier and a head noun；⑧ noun phrase containing an indefinite pronoun，a generic quantifier and a head noun. The formations are instantiated as follows：

（8）NPmod + det（ + mod）　　　　历史上面已经存在的这种有地域特色的文化

NPpos + mod　　　　　　　　她的委托声明

NPpos + det（ + mod）　　　你这房子的情况

NP（mod + ）det + cp　　　末尾那两句话；这几个条件

NPcp + mod　　　　　　　　1908 万元补偿款；末尾两句话

NPmod + g-q　　　　　　　　之后所发生的一系列事情

NPpos + mod + uni-q　　　　曹雪芹的《红楼梦》里每句话

NPind + g-q　　　　　　　　某一步棋

Table 4. 6 presents the results of the distributional investigation of these subcategories.

Table 4. 6　Distribution of subcategories of complex noun phrases

	Subcategories	Number	%
1.	NPmod + det（ + mod)	10	4. 6
2.	NPpos + mod	2	0. 9
3.	NPpos + det（ + mod)	1	0. 5
4.	NP（mod + ）det + cp	2	0. 9
5.	NPcp + mod	2	0. 9
6.	NPmod + g-q	2	0. 9
7.	NPpos + mod + uni-q	1	0. 5
8.	NPind + g-q	1	0. 5
	Total	21	9. 7

Within the scope of complex noun phrases, what stands as the unmarked subcategory, in terms of frequency, is the noun phrases that contain one or two modifiers and a demonstrative determiner (4. 6%). If all the noun phrases that contain a demonstrative determiner are put together in one group and those that do not embrace a demonstrative determiner in a separate group, the members in the former group still outnumber those in the latter. This squares with the observation of simple noun phrases: the forms that contain a demonstrative determiner have the strongest tendency to appear in TOP. Again, one instance of indefinite noun

47

phrase is found. This case, together with the case found in simple noun phrases, blemishes the assumption that topics must be definite (Li and Thompson 1976; Tsao 1977/1995:39).

To further pursue the question why, compared to simple noun phrases, complex noun phrases are, in the main, non-prototypical forms fulfilling the role of CIP topics, we need to turn to the iconic aspect of language. Cognitively, a language has an imitative character (Ungerer and Schmid 1996/2001; Leech and Short 1981/2001; Croft and Cruse 2004/2006; Hopper and Traugott 1993/2001). Onomatopoeic words, for instance, are an illustration of iconic properties of linguistic sounds. Words like *cuckoo*, *bang* in English, "乒乓", "咔嚓" in Chinese and *giseigo* in Japanese are some of the classic examples. Diagrammatic iconicity is seen in Caesar's famous statement 'Veni, vidi, vici' (I came, I saw, I conquered) in which order of mention mirrors order of action described (Hopper and Traugott 2001:26). It also can be understood as conforming to the principle of iconic sequencing. In addition, other iconic phenomena are recognized. Consider the following paired clauses cited from Ungerer and Schmid (2001:252):

(9) a. This guy is getting on my nerves.
  b. This aggressively impertinent egghead is getting on my nerves.

The subject noun phrase in (9a) contains two components: *this* and *guy*. The subject noun phrase in (9b) contains four components: *this*, *aggressively*, *impertinent* and *egghead*. Though the two noun phrases may have the same referent, they differ in terms of the length of linguistic materials. Such difference is congruent with the difference in the amount of information provided by the expressions. The correspondence between formal complexity and cognitive complexity is termed iconic quantity. This provides the basis on which complex noun phrases serving as CIP topics are cognitively interpreted. Demanding much attention and processing efforts, these noun phrases, due to their formal complexity, are restricted from occupying the initial or near initial position in a clause and from becoming prototypical subcategories. This is in compliance with the principle of end-weight as well (cf. Quirk et al. 1985:323; 1039-1040). The observation hence represents a challenge to Jin's (1998) viewpoint of front-weight principle in Chinese. In his comparative study of word order between Chinese and

English, Jin argues that different from the end-weight principle regulating word order in English, "the structural principle influencing the linear word ordering in modern Chinese should be the 'front-weight' principle". He points out that the front-weight principle in Chinese is primarily embodied by topic structures at clausal level in that these structures are canonical, frequent and basic and that the topic is a fronted constituent. The data Jin uses are selected from diverse sources that belong to different genres. They are either cited from other scholars coping with language from different angles, such as syntax or translation, or taken from written texts like magazine articles and newspaper reports. Neglecting the factor of data sources—it is uncertain whether or not the difference between Jin's data source and mine has caused the rift between his argument and the results revealed here—it is hard to treat his claim as valid in the present study. Accordingly, cognitive complexity explains the non-prototypicality of complex noun phrases playing the role of CIP topics.

4.4.3　Demonstratives: a neglected category

Demonstratives functioning as CIP topics have barely dealt with previously in the literature. They are singled out as a separate category in this study so that a deep insight into their features will be gained.

Topicalized demonstratives are used for definite reference. They are simple in form and syntactically constitute the patient argument in CIPT clauses. These words have a frequency, though, as low as 20 and account for only 9.22% of the data. This appears to be a paradox judging by the properties unique to CIP topics and by the principle of end-weight. Indeed, all the demonstratives in TOP found in the corpus data are used anaphorically to refer to something mentioned in the previous discourse. One special point is that the antecedents of these elements are often a clause or a sequence of clauses. Consider the following examples:

（10）那法律为什么不规定兄弟姐妹是第一顺序继承人/<u>这我也不知道</u>/

（11）……所以走的时候/文化界想要留我的那个力量非常非常大/所以走得非常非常地困难/<u>那个是在开始时候没有想到的</u>/

The demonstrative "这" in instance (10) refers ananphorically to the entire clause that goes ahead of the unlined CIPT clause. The item "那个" in (11) refers back to the three continuous clauses that precede the CIPT clause. Comparatively, the processing of the items gets complicated. Sometimes the antecedent of a demonstrative is not directly identified. Consider:

(12) 我们可以在一般的艺术技巧上来分析《红楼梦》的语言技巧、性格刻画/
<u>这个呢其他作品其实都还有</u>/但是这么一种宏伟的内在结构是其他作品
不太有的了

For the expression "这个"[1] in (12), there is no straightforward interpretation. A hearer has to run through in mind three entities coded by such noun phrases as "艺术技巧", "语言技巧" and "性格刻画" before finally arriving at the interpretation that the demonstrative refers back to "艺术技巧". An alternative interpretation is that "这个" refers back to "语言技巧" and "性格刻画" because the two items are details subservient to the general item "艺术技巧". In this case, the two segments, chronically closer, become the antecedent of the demonstrative. Its processing is therefore more complicated when more time and attention are required to retrieve information about its referent from memory. Being cognitively non-economic may be the reason why topicalized demonstratives are less prototypical than noun phrases.

Another phenomenon worth mentioning is that the 'near' demonstratives like "这/这些", "这样" and "这个" far outnumber the 'distant' demonstratives like "那" or "那个". The following table displays the distribution of different demonstratives in the corpus data:

Table 4.7 Distribution of different demonstratives

	Demonstratives		umber	%
	Near	Distant		
1.	这个		10	4.6
2.	这		6	2.8

---

① "这个" and "那个" are classified as pronouns in Liu (2002:170) though "个" is often considered a classifier (Wu and Cheng 1981:232; Zhang 1982:13; Li and Thompson 1981:104). Following Liu, "这个" and "那个" are treated as demonstratives rather than classifier phrases when they are not used as determiners.

	Demonstratives		umber	%
	Near	Distant		
3.	这些		1	0.5
4.	这样		1	0.5
5.		那个	2	0.9
	Total		20	9.2

The two kinds of demonstratives, however, do not differ in their use for anaphoric reference as shown in the above examples. Of the 'near' demonstratives, "这个" is most frequently used.

In his well-known study of topic continuity or topicality as termed later, Givon (1983) holds that "the more disruptive, surprising, discontinuous or hard to process a topic is, the more coding material must be assigned to it". Continuous topical referents—most commonly coded as zero or anaphoric pronouns—must be considered the unmarked referent-coding device whereas full noun phrases are used for the markedness situation and are used to code discontinuous referents (Givon 1995b:50-52). With respect to topic identification, Givon (1983) uses a scale as presented below to illustrate the difference in accessibility status between zero anaphora or pronouns and noun phrases:

(13) Most continuous / accessible topic

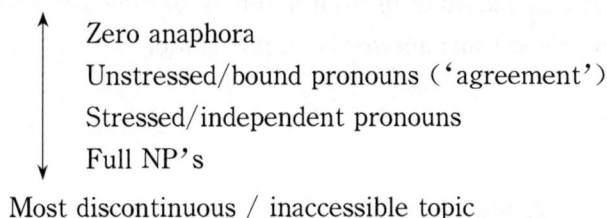

        Zero anaphora

        Unstressed/bound pronouns ('agreement')

        Stressed/independent pronouns

        Full NP's

Most discontinuous / inaccessible topic

For Givon, pronouns, unstressed / bound or stressed / independent, rank higher than full NP's in the scale. However, according to the present study, noun phrases dramatically outnumber demonstratives in their capacity as CIP topics. More importantly, anaphoric reference designated by noun phrases is no less intense than that designated by demonstratives as detailed later in chapter 6. Since anaphoric reference presupposes that information coded by the current referring constituent is not new, it is safe to say that the referents coded by topicalized noun phrases are highly recoverable. Compared to demonstratives, noun phrases are, in terms of frequency, more unmarked. They are eligible for the role of clause topic and even preferred to play that role. In some degree, this proves Givon's claim to be limited. Meanwhile, it underpins the claim made by Pan Wenguo (1997:348-350) that pronouns are less frequently used than nouns in Chinese whereas nouns are preferably used in place of pronouns even when repetition is involved. If repetition is to be avoided, ellipsis rather than a pronoun will be turned to.

4.4.4 Embedded clauses

An embedded clause construction forms a constituent of a matrix clause or main clause. In a topic structure, an embedded clause functioning as CIP topic forms the complement of the matrix verb or of a relevant verb in the comment and topicalized from the post-verbal position, i.e., position internally within V-bar. Xu and Liu (1998:239) hold that a clause playing the role of topic even can be considered a nominal constituent. This is true if we agree on Palmer's thought (1981:198) in the effect that

the intension of an expression, that is to say, is precisely what it is that allows us to 'pick out' the extension of that expression in any possible world. The distinction can now be extended to sentences. The extension of a sentence can be seen as the state of affairs, etc., to which it refers. What then is its intension? The usual answer is 'a proposition'.

As an example, Consider:

(14) a. 他考虑了很久我知道/
     b. 他考虑了很久我知道 >> 他考虑了很久

Example (14a) is a matrix clause. The underlined part in the clause is the embedded clause moved into the initial position from the position succeeding the matrix verb "知道" and leaves a gap there. The expression as a whole plays the role of internal argument in the semantic structure of the matrix clause.

Semantically，the proposition or intension that the matrix clause contains presupposes the proposition or intension contained in the embedded clause. This relationship can be represented as in （14b），where the sign "＞＞" symbolizes "presuppose". Extensionally，the embedded clause denotes a fact in the actual world and has a definite reference.

When the embedded clause is an interrogative，the structure itself presupposes propositions （Yule，1996：28-29；He 1999：224-225）. For example，in tokens such as the following：

（15）a. 我后面是谁我没去看/
　　　 b. 我后面是谁＞＞ 我后面有人
（16）a. 这孩子具体有没有我不清楚/
　　　 b. 这孩子（他）具体有没有＞＞（（他）有孩子 ∨（他）没有孩子）

The embedded clause in TOP in （15a） is a wh-question construction while that in （16a） a yes-no question construction. Both of them constitute the internal argument of the relevant matrix verbs. The embedded question in （15a） can be analyzed as presupposing that as represented in （15b），"我后面有人" is assumed to be true. What is in question is the identity of the person "someone"（人）behind me—the participant engaged in the state of affairs—rather than the whole situation. Since the state of affairs is specified，the wh-question in TOP has a definite interpretation. Turning to （16a），the matrix verb "清楚" in this case is equivalent to the verb "知道". （16b） shows that the yes-no question presupposes that "（他）有孩子" or "（他）没有孩子"（"he has a child" or "he does not have a child"）. Either the first presupposed proposition or the second is assumed to be true，they both denote a specific fact in the real world and have a definite reference. Put differently，what is questioned originally is which presupposition can be treated as true. Whichever is the fact，then，the definiteness is not affected. This brings us to the question why there are only 15 instances of embedded clauses in TOP accounting for 6.9% of the data. The answer seems obvious when cognitive factor is taken into consideration. Other things being equal，the complex structural size is believed，in this study，to be mainly responsible for the fact that embedded clauses are much less frequently used than noun phrases even though they are viewed as nominal units. As far as structure is concerned, embedded clauses resemble complex noun phrases in the sense that they are long and heavy in form. Correspondingly, they take more time and attention to process. When appearing in the initial position in topic structures, these constituents are hence subject to cognitive restrictions and become a non-prototype category. From this perspective, Xu and Liu's viewpoint as mentioned above is one-sided and misleading to a certain extent.

4.4.5 Apposition constructions

Apposition constructions used as CIP topics are diverse in morphological forms though they are unexceptionally comprised of two units. As shown earlier in Table 4.1, some consist of two noun phrases as in "养老院这个制度". Some consist of a verb phrase and a noun phrase like "装错房子这样的事情". Sometimes the appositives are realized as an embedded clause plus a noun phrase such as "钥匙能互开这样的事". Occasionally, a pronoun and a noun phrase comprise such a construction as "它这个山水画". It is not rare that a citation is used as one of the appositives as in "'丁克'这个词". Most of the constructions, in spite of their formal differences, meet the three conditions for full apposition (Quirk et al. 1985:1302): i) each of the appositives can be separately omitted without affecting the acceptability of the sentence; ii) each fulfils the same syntactic function in the resultant sentences; iii) presumably, there is no difference between the original sentence and either of the resultant sentences in extralinguistic reference. Whatever kind of form an apposition construction may be in, the second appositive is consistently a noun phrase such that the entire construction is nominalized. On top of that, there is a strong tendency for a demonstrative determiner to appear in the noun phrase. This phenomenon agrees with the phenomena observed earlier in section 4.4.2.1 and 4.4.2.2 where simple and complex noun phrases are examined. Namely, expressions that contain a demonstrative determiner occur most frequently within the scopes of those two types of phrases respectively. Table 4.8 illustrates the distribution of apposition constructions whose second appositive contains a demonstrative determiner, in comparison with the distribution of all the apposition constructions put together.

	Number	%
Apposition constructions whose 2nd appositive contains a demonstrative determiner	10	4. 6
Total of apposition constructions	13	6. 0

Out of the total 13 apposition constructions, there are 10 instances in which a demonstrative determiner is used in the second appositive. In this way, definite reference of the whole appositional constituent is assured to the greatest extent. Consider:

（17）养老院这个制度能不能推行开/

（18）装错房子这样的事情完全是可以避免的/

In (17), the referent of the first appositive noun phrase is not specific. It can be either "nursing homes in general" or "system". When co-referred to by the second appositive noun phrase, the referent is defined and becomes evident and the appositional constituent has a definite interpretation. The two appositives in (18) belong to different syntactic classes. According to Quirk et al. (1985:1303), elements like these stand in weak apposition. The verb phrase "装错房子" refers to or describes an event and the noun phrase denotes the same event for clarification. A parallel can be drawn between (18) and a case where the first appositive is an embedded clause. Consider the following instance:

（19）钥匙能互开这样的事并没有签入合同/

The extension of the clause appositive "钥匙能互开" is an event which is denoted again and further clarified by the noun phrase appositive "这样的事". Quite different from Chinese, in English, the order of the appositives in such an apposition construction—regardless of its syntactic role—is just the reverse: the noun phrase appears first (ibid:1320-1321). What lies behind the difference merits separate discussion and is not to be dealt with here.

When the first appositive is a proper noun, a book / magazine title or a citation，a demonstrative determiner does not have to appear in the second appositive. For example，in clauses such as the follwing.

(20) 连云港老家我们都去了/

(21)《读书》杂志是很多老头办的

the geographical name "连云港" in (20) straightforwardly refers to an individual place and has a definite reference. The noun phrase "老家" is a defining appositive that provides specific information about the place denoted according to the context. In (21)，the title "读书"，similar to a proper noun，refers to an entity of a unique type in the real world. The appositive bare noun "杂志" provides specific information about the referent and obtains a paraphrase relation with the first appositive. In both cases，despite the absence of a demonstrative determiner，the apposition construction has a definite reference.

Complex in form and requiring much cognitive effort，apposition constructions as a whole do not fit the clause initial position. They are therefore infrequently used in the corpus data in much the same way as embedded clauses are.

4.4.6 Classifier phrases

Classifier phrases are expressions headed by a classifier. They are different in forms：some comprise a demonstrative determiner and a classifier；others comprise a numeral and a classifier；still others comprise a demonstrative determiner，a numeral and a classifier. Classifier phrases are often used to modify a noun and form part of the noun phrase. In this case，the head noun may be dropped if it refers back to an entity mentioned earlier in the previous discourse. What remains then is the classifier phrase only. Consider：

(22) a. 那九个我们就带走了/

　　 b. 我们县里十个人/我是其中一个盖章碰到问题的……他们两个就告诉我说/你不行/你家里还有问题没查清楚/我们还要到上海去作调查/那九个我们就带走了/

In (22a)，the initial definite classifier phrase "那九个" is a topicalized constituent. Syntactically it is controlled by the verb phrase "带走" and forms its internal argument. Obviously the head noun it modifies is dropped such that the referent of the expression is not clear. In (22b), when the previous discourse of the CIPT clause is provided, the antecedent of the dropped element is recovered as "人" from the noun phrase "十个人" and the referent of the classifier phrase is "the other nine people out of the ten". The interpretation of the classifier phrase hence relies much on the context. Seemingly eligible for the role of clause topic in every respect, semantic non-autonomy restrains classifier phrases from occurring alone, especially when their antecedent is a sequence of clauses away from their current occurrence as in (22b). Thus they become a peripheral category accounting for only 2.8% of the corpus data.

4.4.7 Verb phrases

It is pointed out earlier that verb phrases functioning as CIP topics are in fact para-arguments. Statistical examination of the corpus reveals 5 tokens of such phrases accounting for 2.3% of the data. They are the most infrequent class of units and form a marginal category. Analysis made in section 1.1 shows that a verb phrase has the potentiality of being converted into a constituent of another type or category. Consider the following instance cited from section 1.1:

（23）量房子我不可能不知道/

The agent of the verb "量" does not appear when the utterance is made. If it is supposedly added as in (24a), what is topicalized becomes an embedded clause. Or further, if the event described by the verb phrase is supposedly co-referred to by a noun phrase in apposition as in (24b), what is topicalized then becomes an apposition construction. In both cases, the topicalized constituent is nominal. In this sense, the topicalized verb phrase "量房子" in (23) can be analyzed as an expression simplified or shortened from the corresponding embedded clause or apposition construction for brevity.

（24）a. 他们量房子我不可能不知道/
　　　b. 量房子这件事我不可能不知道/

Besides the instance above, all the other four instances found in the corpus data show that the verb phrase in TOP can be converted into an embedded clause when the dropped agent is added according to the context as in（25）～（28）below：

（25）a. 怎么捅破的不知道/
       b. 我怎么捅破的不知道
（26）a. 你说具体是姐姐还是妹妹我不大清楚/
       b. 你说她们具体是姐姐还是妹妹我不大清楚
（27）a. 出这种事开发商也实在是想不到/
       b. 业主出这种事开发商也实在是想不到
（28）a. 把自己的村委会告上法庭这是洪水坤不愿意看到的/
       b. 村民把自己的村委会告上法庭这是洪水坤不愿意看到的

Instance (28a) is different from (26a), (27a) and (28a) in that the verb phrase in TOP becomes the antecedent of the succeeding demonstrative determiner "这". The two units denote the same event in the real world. "这" is treated as a twin topic in the present study. Syntactically both elements are coreferential with the post-verbal gap. Drawing upon Hockett, (28a) can be analyzed as a layered topic structure. Namely, if the topicalized verb phrase is omitted, the remaining expression can stand alone as a topic structure. Then the demonstrative "这" will still play the role of CIP topic.

Conversely, some embedded clauses and apposition constructions found in the corpus can be reduced to verb phrases while the resultant topic structures remain well-formed. Consider：

（29）a. 装错房子这样的事情完全是可以避免的/
       b. 装错房子完全是可以避免的
（30）a. 这纸什么时候捅破的也不知道/
       b. 什么时候捅破的也不知道

Examples (29) and (30) provide further evidence for our assumption that verb phrases may have derived from embedded clauses or apposition constructions. Such analyses help to answer the question why a verb phrase, as a non-pure argument or para-argument, can be treated as an argument and in turn as a CIP topic. Ideationally describing an event allows a verb phrase to play the semantic role that usually an embedded clause or apposition construction, i. e. , a nominal constituent can play. This may be considered one of the manifestations typical of the topic-prominent Chinese language. On the other hand, verb phrases are subject to restrictions since what they denote does not represent felicitous participants engaged in the activities described by relevant verbs. When they compete with embedded clauses or apposition constructions for the role of topic, embedded clauses gain the upper hand with the highest frequency among the three. Verb phrases rank second. Apposition constructions, in the form of APvp $+\mathrm{np_{det}}$, rank third with only 3 occurrences.

4.5　A comparison between Chinese and English

Turning attention to categories of phrases in TOP in English, Birner and Ward (1998: 45-47) diverge from other researchers. Under their view, topicalization is not limited to noun phrases. Major phrasal categories that can be topicalized include:

(31) a. NP: One of these rugs Chambers delivered to Harry Dexter White.
    b. PP: For that last bold assertion there are no statistics.
    c. VP:... and pass I did.
    d. AP: Humble they may be. But daft they ain't.

(Birner and Ward 1998:45-46)

Judging by the definition of CIP topic set in chapter 1 in this study, however, only the topicalized noun phrase in (31a) fits the purpose of the comparison being made at the moment. Specifically, "one of these rugs" is governed by the verb "delivered". It constitutes the internal argument of the verb. This instance is most representative of topicalization in English as found in pertinent studies. No topicalized phrase of the other three categories in (31b)～(31d) denotes an entity playing the patient role in the activity or event described by the relevant verb. They are therefore ignored here. Such phrases are also ignored in Gregory and Michaelis' (2001) study. This is where their study and mine are juxtaposed. Going through the TOP examples Gregory and Michaelis uses, it is obvious that the linguistic units playing the role of clause topic are exclusively nominal and pronominal forms as shown in the following:

(32) ... And that sort of thing I enjoy.

(33) One of them I would leave unsupervised any time, any place, anywhere.

(34) That I didn't ever understand.

(Gregory and Michaelis 2001)

Namely, noun phrases and demonstratives in TOP are most common in spoken English though difference in their distribution is not revealed. This is true with instances used by other researchers dealing with topicalization in English. One interesting similarity is that personal pronouns, as in my own corpus data, do not occur in TOP in Gregory and Michaelis' study. Neither do they occur elsewhere in the literature.

4.6　Summary

This chapter investigates categories of units that can function as CIP topics. A corpus-based exploration reveals that there are six such categories: NP, DEM, EC, AP, CP and VP. These categories do not exhibit even distribution in the data, though. Rather, members of NP have the highest frequency. They make up an overwhelming majority of the data and form the prototype category. Other categories make up either a minor or a marginal proportion of the data and are non-prototype. When members of NP category are subcategorized and examined, simple and complex noun phrases are distinguished. The former ones far outnumber the latter. Within the scope of simple noun phrases, units that contain a demonstrative determiner or a modifier and bare nouns are shown to be the prototype sub-categories. When the distribution of categories and subcategories is delved into, such factors as reference status, initial position in the topic structure and structural size are found to make a difference.

Chapter 5　Syntactic patterns
of CIPT clauses

5.1　Introduction

　　In the course of collecting CIP topics, we find that the process of picking such topics actually involves a scrutiny of the structures that the topicalized constituent forms a part of. The research on CIP topics is intertwined with that on CIPT clauses to such an extent that the study of CIP topics is unlikely to be systematic and exhaustive when syntax is not taken into account. CIPT clause patterns touched upon in the literature to date come to no more than ten types. In the present study, however, the patterns are for the first time found to be very diverse and amount to more than twenty.

　　In this chapter a thorough research is conducted on syntactic patterns of CIPT clauses. Distribution of different patterns is probed into, described and explained. Prototype patterns are empirically presented. In addition, based on written Chinese, a separate mini-sized corpus of CIPT clauses is created. Patterns of the clauses and their distribution are examined and discussed. The research then extends to an investigation of the English translations of these clauses on the basis of a further separately created corpus. A brief sketch of the organization of this chapter is as follows. Section 5.2 presents research questions. Section 5.3 describes research design. Section 5.4 explains how the corpus data are coded generally as well as specifically and analyzed statistically. It then presents and discusses the results of the analyses. Section 5.5 compares the occurrence of CIPT clauses in spoken Mandarin with that of topicalization constructions in spoken English. In section 5.6, a parallel study of CIPT clause patterns in written Chinese is conducted based on data collected from two drama texts: *Teahouse* by Lao She and *Uncle Doggie's Nirvana* by Jin Yun. Finally, section 5.7 examines the syntactic forms adopted in the English translations of CIPT clauses in question and discusses the gap between them from the angle of informational structure and discoursal association.

5.2 Research questions

This chapter aims to address the following questions:

(1) What syntactic patterns do CIPT clauses present in the spoken data? And how do the patterns distribute? What is /are the prototype pattern (s)?

(2) In what ways is the occurrence of CIPT clauses in spoken Mandarin different from that of topicalization constructions in spoken English?

(3) What syntactic patterns do CIPT clauses present in the written data? How do the patterns distribute? How do they differ from those in the spoken data?

(4) What patterns do the English translations of CIPT clauses under discussion present? How do the patterns distribute in the relevant data?

5.3 Design

In order to address the first question, the research is designed to code the data by hand for a start so that a statistical analysis will be made later. Data coding is conducted on two levels: general and specific. On the general level, types of CIPT clauses are identified and coded. On the specific level, subtypes of CIPT clauses within each type are further identified and coded. When coding at both levels is finished, Excel 2003 is used to automatically process CIPT clauses for categorization and sub-categorization. Lastly, results of analyses are reported and discussed.

When comparing occurrence of CIPT clauses in spoken Mandarin and that of topicalization constructions in spoken English, I avail myself of the findings in Gregory and Michaelis's (2001) research for the English part rather than myself conducting an independent study in the same regard.

To address the third question, written data are collected from Chinese literary works and a separate corpus is created. Syntactic patterns of CIPT clauses in this corpus are investigated categorically as well.

To address the forth question, a translation study is conducted. In a sense, the study forms a sub-study on a small scale building on examinations in the previous sections. The English translations of the written Chinese data are collected and statistical analyses are made. Accordingly, disparity between CIPT clauses in Chinese and their English translations is unraveled and discussed.

5.4 Syntactic patterns of CIPT clauses

5.4.1 Data coding

Different from coding in chapter 4, coding in this chapter refers to the process of sorting the syntactic patterns of CIPT clauses and labeling them with capital letters. If necessary, a number or symbol is used. Qualitative analysis is thus involved. The data used here are those already coded for the investigation of CIP topics in the previous chapter. As mentioned above, the process comprises two phases—general coding and specific coding. The two phases are necessary so that classification and sub-classification of the clause patterns can be carried out automatically.

5.4.1.1 General coding: types of CIPT clauses

General coding is the process of identifying and labeling the general syntactic type of a CIPT clause. It is pointed out previously that CIPT clauses are of different patterns. Some examples discussed in Chapter 1 are repeated here to illustrate how a token is assigned a general code. Consider:

(1) 我后面是谁我没去看/
(2) 这首歌演唱得很有弹性/

The common ground of the clauses above is that the main verb in the comment functions as a two-place predicate and takes two arguments. The post-verbal argument position is occupied by a gap. The initial constituent, i. e., the CIP topic, is coreferential with the gap. The major difference between the two topic structures is that the agent of the verb is overt in example (1) while covert in (2). The former is coded as type **A** and the latter type **B**. In addition, the appearance of... *shi*... *de* construction, or its alternative forms like *shi*...

63

and...de in some CIPT clauses makes their coding much more complicated. As an example, consider:

(3) 两本书是同时写的/

The reason why example (3) is treated as a CIPT clause is given in detail in section 1.1. What distinguishes it from clauses (1) and (2) is the use of the *shi...de* construction in the comment. Though the copula "是" is optional, the presence of the particle "的" is a must in the context.

On many occasions the two elements *shi* and *de* do not have to occur simultaneously. Each can stand alone without the companionship of the other. Consider the following:

(4) 搬迁这事是在 2004 年底就已经确定了/
(5) 这个历史你没有办法改写的/

The constituents in TOP "搬迁这事" and "这个历史" are co-referencial with the post-verbal gaps in both topic structures. They are governed respectively by the verbs "确定" and "改写". The particle *de* is omitted in (4) while *shi* is omitted in (5). Further, variations of the clauses will still be acceptable if *shi* is not present in example (4) and *de* not in (5). Put differently, the *shi...de* construction can occur either in complete form or in elliptic form without affecting the meaning of a clause. It even can be dropped as a whole without altering the clause meaning, either.

Principles hence abided by when clauses like instances (3), (4) and (5) are coded as follows: (a) a clause is coded as type **C** as long as the *shi...de* construction appears in it. This principle applies, no matter whether the construction is used in complete form or in elliptic form, or whether the element *shi* is used for emphasis or as a linking verb; (b) for cases in which the *shi...de* construction, either in complete or elliptic form, can be omitted as a whole without changing the clause meaning, the clauses are marked with the "♯" symbol.

A closer observation reveals that distinctions can be drawn among examples (3), (4) and (5). A parallel is found between (3) and (4) in that the agent is covert in both of them. Example (5) differs from (3) and (4) with the agent "你" of the verb being used though it does not have a specific reference in the context. If the syntactic construction *shi... de* is ignored for a while, the distinction between (3) and (5) or between (4) and (5) would be similar to that between type A clauses and type B clauses. The parallel between (3) and (4) would then bring them together under type B. Therefore, within type C, a further distinction is made. Clauses in which the agent is overt as in (5) are coded as type CA. Clauses in which the agent is covert as in (3) or (4) are coded as type CB.

As far as clauses of type CA are concerned, the position of *shi* is not fixed. For example, in clauses such as the following:

(6) 这种巨大的变化是你们两位都没有曾经想到过的/
(7) 这个情况她是明知的/

the element *shi* obviously can appear either before the agent or after it. Positional variation of this kind is ignored in the phase of general coding at the moment but will be dealt with in the phase of specific coding.

The flexible position of *shi* brings to attention the question about the element's function. Some scholars believe that the use of the *shi... de* construction is to achieve emphasis or to strengthen affirmation (Wu 1985:307; Zhang 1982:132; Wu and Cheng 1981:224, 282). Li and Thompson (1981:500) argue that the construction serves the function of placing the agent noun phrase in focus when the topic of a clause is the direct object. One of the examples they use is cited as follows:

(8) a. Zhei ge zhengce shi ta tuijian de.
   b. * Zhei ge zhengce bei ta tuijian le.

To their understanding, when the focus is on the agent of the transitive action verb *tuijian*, clause (8a) should be used rather than (8b). According to the current study, such an assumption is limited. With respect to instance (6), the agent "你们两位", though immediately succeeding the element shi, is not the focus. Prosodic examination reveals that "你们两位" is unstressed whereas the verb phrase "想到" is the intonation nucleus. The latter rather than the former thus constitutes the focus. From the angle of informational structure, shi functions to signal the upcoming constituent where the focus lies. By the same token, in instance (7) where the element *shi* is positioned after the agent, the verb phrase "明知" is stressed as prosody shows and hence becomes the focus. It functions to indicate that the focus is about to appear. In cases like (6), (7) and (8a), *shi* can be omitted and the resultant clauses are still sound while the foci remain unchanged. Even in a clause in which the agent is covert, like (3), the function of *shi* is just the same. In that case, the adverb "同时" becomes the focus. A broader explanation proposed here is: no matter where it locates, *shi* serves the function of signaling that the focus is to follow. Whatever semantic or grammatical role the focus plays, *shi* can come either immediately before it or the two can be separated with some other elements standing in between them.

When general coding is finished, all the data are classified. The matching relationship between a token and the code it bears is checked and assured. The same is done with the omission symbol "♯" assigned to some of type C clauses. Then the data are arranged in an alphabetical order by the computer according to the codes that index their syntactic types. Each type is extracted from the corpus, created as a sub-corpus. Three sub-corpora are therefore established for the three types of CIPT clauses: sub-corpora A, B and C. Sub-corpus C is further divided into sub-sub-corpora[①] CA and CB.

5. 4. 1. 2　Specific coding: subtypes and syntactic patterns of CIPT clauses

Specific coding is conducted within each sub-corpus. It refers to the process of identifying and labeling the subtype of each CIPT clause and the syntactic pattern it demonstrates. Factors like recurrence of a syntactic pattern, matrix clause, grammatical object and twin topics are all taken into consideration and embodied in the coding in this phase. What is eventually achieved is sub-classification of the data yielding subtypes of CIPT clauses and relevant syntactic patterns.

- **Recurring syntactic patterns**

It is interesting to note that within each type, one syntactic pattern occurs

---

① For convenience, "sub-corpus (sub-corpora)" will be used later as a cover term for both sub-corpus (sub-corpora) and sub-sub-corpus (sub-sub-corpora).

most frequently. In comparison, all the rest patterns occur only sporadically and become variations of the recurring pattern. Naturally, there are four such patterns with each standing for the type it belongs to. These patterns are considered as prototypes. They are respectively exemplified by (1), (2), (3) and (5) as mentioned above. The subtypes that the patterns fall under are coded respectively as A1, B1, CA1 and CB1. The syntactic patterns for clauses of subtypes A1 and B1 are expressed as "TSV" and "TV" respectively. "T" represents topic. "S" represents grammatical subject that is also agent or actor. In clauses where the copula *shi* is obligotory, namely, when *shi* functions as a linking verb, "S" represents the agent or actor only whereas "T" stands for both topic and subject. "V" always represents the verb that governs the patient argument, i. e. the topic. Since the *shi...de* construction indexed by C can take different forms and the position of "*shi*" is flexible, the syntactic patterns for clauses of subtypes CA1 and CB1 need to be expressed in several different ways. For subtype CA1 clauses, the patterns include T*shi*SV*de*, TS*shi*V*de*, TS*shi*V and TSV*de*. For subtype CB1 clauses, the patterns include T*shi*V*de*, T*shi*V and TV*de*.

- **Matrix clauses**

Matrix clauses in which an embedded clause itself is a topic structure are briefly touched upon in chapter 1. In such cases, there are three possible positions for the matrix clause: initial, medial and final. These positions are respectively designated by subcript numbers "1", "2" and "3". For example, if a matrix clause occupies the initial position as in the following:

(9) 我觉得这个事情我真的不想去做/

It is coded as MC_1. The embedded clause syntactically plays the role of object of the matrix verb "觉得". The topicalized constituent "这个事情" occurs within the boundaries of the embedded clause. Since the embedded constituent in this case is of type A, the subtype of the whole structure is coded as AMC_1. Its syntactic pattern is expressed as MCTSV in which the position of "MC" indicates the initial position that the matrix clause occupies in the entire structure. When the matrix clause occupies the medial position, as shown in (10) below cited from chapter 1, it is coded as MC_2:

（10）（这个）元春（呢）[∨] 小说就告诉你就选进去了／

The embedded topic structure "这个元春呢……就选进去了" is of type B. The topic "元春" together with the topic marker "这个……呢" is separated from the comment "就选进去了" by the matrix clause "小说就告诉你". An element topicalized in such a way is referred to by Shi (2002: 54) as long distance movement. The subtype of the whole topic structure is coded as BMC_2. Its syntactic pattern is expressed as TMCV, in which the position of "MC", in between "T" and "V", stands for the medial position of the matrix clause.

When the matrix clause occupies the final position as in (11) below:

（11）这孩子具体有没有我不清楚／

It is coded as MC_3. Again, the embedded clause is of type B and the subtype of the whole structure is coded as BMC_3. The syntactic pattern is expressed as TVMC. It is interesting to note that, viewed from a different angle, the embedded structure "这孩子具体有没有" in turn forms the CIP topic of the matrix verb "清楚". In this case, the subtype of the entire clause is coded as A1. The syntactic pattern is expressed as TSV in which "T" stands for the embedded topic structure. Example (11) is a case that involves twice coding.

In all the three instances above, the embedded clause remains acceptable if the matrix clause is omitted. This is true whatever syntactic pattern the embedded clause will take.

• **Object**

CIPT clauses containing an object are not rare in the corpus. Yet the semantic relation that the object holds with the relevant verb is of a different kind. In some clauses, the verb is a three-place predicate and takes three arguments that play different semantic roles. Consider the predicate "给" in example (12) below:

（12）房子 t 给了小儿子／

It is clear that the expressions "房子", "小儿子" and a covert element in the position of t are the arguments taken by the verb "给". "房子" and "小儿子"

respectively play the semantic roles of patient and recipient. The covert element plays the role of agent. Syntactically, the patient is fronted and becomes the CIP topic. The recipient remains in the post-verbal position and forms the indirect object. Objects in some other clauses like (13) below are different:

(13) 这个捍虎图啊[∨] t 画了不止一张/

What distinguishes (13) from (12) is that the verb "画" functions as a two-place predicate. Its argument structure specifies that it takes two arguments. Again, the agent argument that performs the act of "画" is covert and leaves a trace between the post-topic marker "啊" and the predicate verb. The patient argument is originally realized by the noun phrase "一张捍虎图". When the head of the noun phrase "捍虎图" is topicalized, it becomes the clause-initial constituent preceded by the pre-topic marker "这个". On the other hand, the classifier phrase "一张", originally the modifier in the noun phrase, remains in the post-verbal position and plays the grammatical role of direct object. With respect to the predicate, "捍虎图" and "一张" are still semantically related and jointly play the role of patient though structurally separated. This phenomenon is termed as argument fission by Liu (2003). Hence neither the semantic nor grammatical roles of "一张" in (13) and "小儿子" in (12) are the same. Yet, when coded, they are both labeled as "O". Both clauses are sub-classified as BO. Their syntactic structures are expressed in the same way as "TVO".

Still another kind of CIPT clauses whose coding is worth mentioning are those described as unusual in section 1.1. The example discussed there is repeated as follows:

(14) 这个木料是谁订的货呀/

It is pointed out earlier that "这个木料" is both topic and subject. The copula "是" functions to link the constituents preceding and succeeding it. The object in this case is the noun phrase that follows the linking verb "是". "货" is the head of the objective noun phrase. Semantically, the topic "这个木料" is governed by the two-place verb "订" occurring in the relative clause. It holds a hyponym-superordinate relation with the head noun "货". "货" is coded as "O". The clause is sub-classified as CAO and its syntactic structure is expressed as T*shi*SV*de*O.

One clause pattern in the corpus is even more unusual. It is given in (15) below:

(15) 这个问题应该讲[∨]我是比较早地提出来的一个/

Though syntactically resembling (14), deviation can be found in the clause as far as semantic relation is concerned. In the expression that functions as the object of the obligatory linking verb "是", the head is a classifier phrase "一个". Clearly, an element succeeding "一个" is dropped. According to the previous discourse, "一个" is shortened from "一个学者". Thus the classifier phrase can be understood as an explanation of the agent "我" that performs the act of "提出来". As for the topic "这个问题", it is coreferential with the gap behind the verb phrase and plays the semantic role of patient. Unlike (14), in this instance, the topic and the objective classifier phrase are not semantically related. For convenience, the head of the objective phrase is still recorded as "O". However, the clause is sub-classified as CAO' with the apostrophe indicating its deviation from CAO. Its syntactic structure is expressed as TS*shi*V*de*O.

- **Twin CIP topics**

The phenomenon of twin CIP topics is infrequent in the corpus data. It is made clear in section 4.4.7 that when two elements are referred to as twin CIP topics, they are, while having the same referents, simultaneously governed by the same verb. Consider the following example:

(16) 像元迎探惜[∨]她们都是有可能选进宫的/

Here the noun phrase "元迎探惜" is the antecedent of the pronoun "她们". The two constituents refer to the same entities in the novel text. Both are coreferential with the post-verbal gap. They play the same semantic role of patient in relation to the act described by the verb "选" and form twin topics. Yet the two are not in apposition because there is a perceivable prosodic pause between them according to the audio-recording. A closer observation reveals that the comment "她们都是有可能选进宫的" can stand alone as an independent topic structure if the pre-topic marker "像" and the topic "元迎探惜" are dropped. When this occurs, "她

们" still stands as a CIP topic. This analysis is compatible with the claim made by Xu and Liu (1998:51) to the effect that a topic structure can hold two or more main topics. Example (17) is cited from Xu and Liu (1998:61) as evidence:

(17) 小张,这件事,我认为[ ]办不了[ ]。

Both "小张" and "这件事" are the main topics of the clause. The disparity between (16) and (17) is that in (17), "小张" and "这件事" are respectively coreferential with the preverbal and post-verbal gaps in the embedded clause and play different semantic roles of agent and patient. To give prominence to its syntactic resemblance to subtype CB1, instance (16) is sub-classified as CB1'. Its syntactic pattern is represented as TT*shi*V*de*. A simliar kind of topic structure may exhibit a somewhat different syntactic pattern. Take (18) for instance:

(18) 你比如河北唐山开平区刘官屯煤矿的 12・7 重大责任事故ᵛ 这个案件那么我们挂牌督办/

The agent is overt here. The element "你比如" is treated as topic marker. The noun phrases "河北唐山开平区刘官屯煤矿的 12・7 重大责任事故" and "这个案件" form twin topics. The clause is coded as A1' and its syntactic pattern is recorded as TTSV. Sometimes the twin units may belong to quite different syntactic categories—one is a verb phrase and the other a pronominal form—as shown earlier in section 4.4.7. Yet the syntactic pattern is described in the same spirit.

When specific coding of data is finished, all tokens are subtyped and their syntactic patterns recorded. The matching relationship between a token and the codes assigned to it is checked until correct coding is assured to the greatest extent.

5.4.2 Syntactic patterns identified

When all the tokens in the four sub-corpora are coded, the syntactic patterns identified can be sorted out as shown in Table 5.1 below. Meanwhile, the subtypes under which the patterns subsume are also sorted out.

Table 5.1 Syntactic patterns of CIPT clauses identified in the corpus data

Types		Subtypes		Syntactic patterns	
A		1.	A1	1.	TSV
		2.	A1'	2.	TTSV
		3.	AMC_1	3.	MCTSV
		4.	AMC_2	4.	TMCSV
		5.	AO	5.	TSVO
B		6.	B1	6.	TV
		7.	BMC_1	7.	MCTV
		8.	BMC_2	8.	TMCV
		9.	BMC_3	9.	TVMC
		10.	BO	10.	TVO
C	CA	11.	CA1	11.	T*shi*SV*de*
				12.	TS*shi*V*de*
				13.	TS*shi*V
				14.	TSV*de*
		12.	CA1'	15.	TT*shi*SV*de*
		13.	$CAMC_1$	16.	MC T*shi*SV*de*
		14.	CAO	17.	T*shi*SV*de*O
		15.	CAO'	18.	TS*shi*V*de*O
	CB	16.	CB1	19.	T*shi*V*de*
				20.	T*shi*V
				21.	TV*de*
		17.	CB1'	22.	TT*shi*V*de*
		18.	$CBMC_1$	23.	MCT*shi*V*de*
		19.	$CBMC_2$	24.	TMC*shi*V*de*
		20.	$CBMC_3$	25.	TV*de*MC
		21.	CBO	26.	T*shi*V*de*O
		22.	$CBOMC_1$	27.	MCT*shi*VO

All together there are twenty-two subtypes of CIPT clauses，specifically，twenty-seven patterns，occurring in the spoken data.

Table 5.1，however，does not serve the purpose of this chapter. To investigate distribution of different syntactic patterns，all the data are arranged in a way that automatic processing can be carried out and analyzed in Excel 2003. Table 5.2 below provides a portion of the coded data in sub-corpus CA as a sample.

Table 5.2　Sample of coded data in sub-corpus CA

No.	Types	Sub-types	Syntactic patterns	Omission	sub-cates. of topics	Tokens	Position
1.	CA	CA1	TshiSVde		NPmod	但毕竟人家的不幸是自己的妻子一手造成的/	171922
2.	CA	CA1	TshiSVde		APcit + n	《读书》杂志是很多老头办的/	210608
3.	CA	CA1	TshiSVde	#	NPdet	这个楠木呢是这样的人物才能使用的/	243500
4.	CA	CA1	TshiSV		NPdet	这些话往往都是刚入行不久的新老师才这么说/	310944
5.	CA	CAO'	TSshiVdeO		NPdet	这个问题应该讲ᵛ我是比较早地提出来的一个/	042620
6.	CA	CA1	TshiSVde	#	NPdet	而这个影响可能是没有爱心ᵛ缺乏爱心的老师可能他不会预料到的/	312332
7.	CA	CA1	TshiSVde	#	NPdet + mod	这么一种宏伟的内在结构是其他作品不太有的了/	133455
8.	CA	CA1'	TTshiSVde	#	VP⇔DEM	把自己的村委会告上法庭ᵛ这是洪水坤不愿意看到的/	181915
9.	CA	CA1	TshiSVde		APpron + np$_{dem+mod}$	它这个山水画是后人临的也好/	061015
10.	CA	CAO	TshiSVdeO		NPdet	这个木料原来是谁定的货呀/	243357
11.	CA	CA1	TshiSVde		NPde	人所有的就是他想要的/	011623
12.	CA	CA1	TshiSVde		NPmod + det	我所有的那种比如比较平等的关系ᵛ比较轻松的生活ᵛ就是我想要的/	011628
13.	CA	CA1	TshiSVde		NPdet	这份赔偿协议是张伟主动提出来要签订的/	141025

73

No.	Types	Sub-types	Syntactic patterns	Omission	sub-cates. of topics	Tokens	Position
14.	CA	CAMC$_1$	MCTshiSVde		NPdet	谁也没有怀疑过这个画最初不是顾恺之画的/	060530
15.	CA	CAO	TshiSVdeO		NPmod	人物画是中国最早发展起来的一个画种/	060908

5.4.3 Results and discussion

This section reports the results of statistical investigation into CIPT clause types and subtypes. Distribution of different syntactic patterns will be presented in the following space. Other features of CIPT clauses are to be examined in detail.

5.4.3.1 Distribution of different types of CIPT clauses

Based on general coding, three types of CIPT clauses are found in the spoken corpus data: A, B and C. Clauses of type C further fall apart into two types: CA and CB. Frequencies of tokens of different types are shown in Table 5.3 below. Their distribution in the corpus is displayed visually in Figure 5.1:

Table 5.3 Distribution of different types of CIPT clauses in the corpus data

	A	B	C		Total
			CA	CB	
N	77	79	31	30	217
%	35.5	36.4	14.3	13.8	100.0

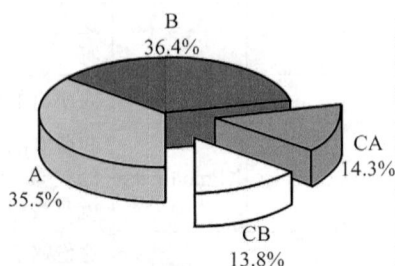

Figure 5.1 Distribution of different types of CIPT clauses in the corpus

According to the graph, tokens of type B account for 36.4% of the pooled data and rank the highest in the corpus. Tokens of type A account for 35.5% and rank second. Tokens of type C, covering CA and CB, account for 28.1% of the pooled data and rank the lowest. The discrepancy between the percentages of type A and B is quite narrow though. The implication is that the tendencies for clauses of types A and B to appear in spoken Mandarin are similarly strong. Their occurrences do not correlate much with the variable of agent—whether it is present or not. The same is true with clauses of types CA and CB since their frequencies are also very close. Apparently the low percentage of type C clauses, compared to those of clauses of types A and B, can be attributed to the presence of the *shi...de* construction or its variation forms that makes the syntax of a topic structure more complicated.

5.4.3.2 Distribution of CIPT clauses of different subtypes

Specific coding yields various subtypes of CIPT clauses in each sub-corpus. Their frequencies in the pooled data are presented in the following tables.

Table 5.4 Distribution of CIPT clauses under type A

	A1	A1'	AMC_1	AMC_2	AO	Total
N	71	1	2	2	1	77
%	32.7	0.5	0.9	0.9	0.5	35.5

Table 5.5 Distribution of CIPT clauses under type B

	B1	BMC1	BMC_2	BMC_3	BO	Total
N	65	5	2	1	6	79
%	30.0	2.3	0.9	0.5	2.8	36.4

Table 5.6 Distribution of CIPT clauses under type CA

	CA1	CA1'	$CAMC_1$	CAO	CAO'	Total
N	25	1	1	3	1	31
%	11.5	0.5	0.5	1.4	0.5	14.3

Table 5. 7　Distribution of CIPT clauses under type CB

	CB1	CB1'	$CBMC_1$	$CBMC_2$	$CBMC_3$	CBO	$CBOMC_1$	Total
N	21	2	2	2	1	1	1	30
%	9.7	0.9	0.9	0.9	0.5	0.5	0.5	13.8

According to tables 5. 4 through 5. 7, five subtypes of CIPT clauses are respectively found in sub-corpus A, B and CA while seven subtypes in sub-corpus CB. In each sub-corpus, the subtype whose pattern recurs most frequently forms the biggest proportion. Such subtypes are A1, B1, CA1 and CB1. The recurring patterns hence become prototypical. Patterns that occur infrequently are non-prototypical.

5. 4. 3. 3　Distribution of prototypical and non-prototypical syntactic patterns

To have a better understanding of the prototypicality of the recurring patterns—the most representative syntactic forms of CIPT clause, their distribution is examined in the pooled data in comparison with that of the non-prototypical patterns put together. The result is shown in Table 5.8 below.

Table 5. 8　Distribution of prototypical and non-prototypical patterns in the pooled data

	A		B		CA		CB		Total
	TSV	Others	TV	others	TshiSVde TSshiVde TSshiV TSVde	others	TshiVde TshiV TVde	others	
N	71	6	65	14	25	6	21	9	217
%	32.7	2.8	30.0	6.5	11.5	2.8	9.7	4.1	100

The graph in Figure 5. 2 below provides a visual representation of distribution on the part of the prototypical patterns in comparison with that of the non-prototypical ones put together in the pooled data.

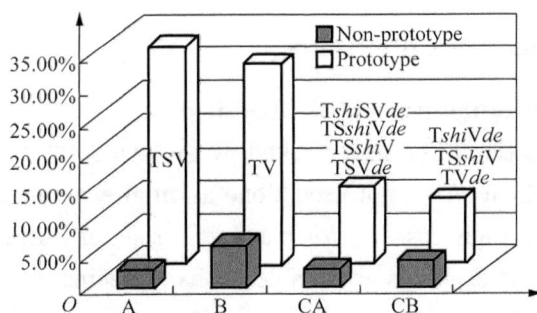

Figure 5. 2   Distribution of prototypical and non-prototypical patterns

Four pairs of bars are drawn to represent tokens in the four sub-corpora. The tall bar in each pair stands for the portion that the prototypical patterns make up in the pooled data. By contrast, the short bar stands for the portion that the non-prototypical patterns jointly make up. Of all the patterns, TSV in sub-corpus A forms the biggest part accounting for 32.7% of the data. TV in sub-corpus B forms the second biggest part accounting for 30.0% of the data. The cluster of patterns in sub-corpus CA including T*shi*SV*de*, TS*shi*V*de*, TS*shi*V and TSV*de* forms the third biggest part accounting for 11.5%. The cluster of patterns in sub-corpus CB including T*shi*V*de*, T*shi*V and TV*de* forms the forth biggest part accounting for 9.7%. In fact, these last two groups of patterns are far less prototypical than TSV and TV in the pooled data although they can be considered prototypical within sub-corpora CA and CB respectively. It is evident that prototypical patterns, taken together, form the lion's share of the data. The remaining non-prototypical patterns as a whole form the minor proportion.

Since the frequency of TSV pattern is higher than that of TV pattern, the tendency for TSV pattern to occur in the corpus is stronger than that for TV pattern. Namely, it is more common for a topic structure to occur when the agent or actor of a verb is used than when they are dropped. The same is true of the two clusters of prototypical patterns in sub-corpora CA and CB. Other things being equal, topic structures in which the agent or actor is present have a stronger tendency to occur than those in which the agent or actor is omitted. Presumably, the syntactic form of a clause becomes complicated when the *shi... de* construction or its variation occurs. Clauses of type C, on the whole, have conditional use restrictions and are less frequent than those of type A and type B.

5. 4. 3. 4　More features of CIPT clauses

• **Clauses marked with the symbol "#" revisited**

Further examination of clauses marked by the symbol "#" reveals that there exist instances in which *shi* is not used alone as an alternative form of the *shi... de* construction. In such cases, *shi* plays the role of suffix. Still, if *shi* is dropped, the resultant clause is acceptable. What remains exhibits a pattern of a subtype that comes under either type A or B. Consider the following:

（19）眼前的事情就算是处理完了/

（20）我觉得可能文学的鉴赏力还是有一些吧/

（21）这个钱我还是还得出的/

The syntactic pattern of (19) is T*shi*V. The noun phrase in TOP "眼前的事情" is coreferencial with the gap following the verb phrase "处理完". The agent of the verb is covert. The element *shi* in this case is not an elliptic form of the *shi... de* construction. Instead, it functions as a suffix added to the verb "算". Lv (1999: 515) holds that *shi* can be present or absent if preceded by "算". In (19), when *shi* is omitted, the clause is not affected either syntactically or semantically. What is left then is a clause of subtype B1 in the pattern of TV. The syntactic pattern of (20) is MCT*shi*VO. The embedded topic structure contains an argument fission construction. The topic "文学的鉴赏力" and the object "一些", though syntactically separated, jointly play the semantic role of patient of the verb "有". *Shi* functions as a suffix but is added here to the adverb "还". It can be omitted without altering the clause meaning either. The remaining clause then will take the syntactic form of MCTVO. Further, if "MC" is omitted, what is left is a TVO pattern. The analysis of *shi* in clause (20) applies to *shi* in (21) though the syntactic pattern of the latter is different. In (21), if *shi* is dropped, the pattern changes from T*shi*SV to the prototype TSV of subtype A1.

An investigation is made into the distribution of clauses bearing the symbol "#" ignoring whether the *shi... de* construction is used in complete or elliptical form and whether *shi* is used as a suffix. The result is shown in the table below.

Table 5. 9　Distribution of clauses marked with " $\sharp$ " in the pooled data

		CA			CB		
	Subtypes	N	%	Subtypes	N	%
Clauses marked with " $\sharp$ "	CA1(13)	13	6.0	CB1(16) CB1'(2) CBMC$_2$(2) CBCBOMC$_1$(1)	21	9.7
Total		31	14.3		30	13.8

The number of clauses marked with " $\sharp$ " in sub-corpus CA amounts to 13. They all come under subtype CA1. Suppose that the *shi...de* construction or *shi* as a suffix is omitted, these clauses will emerge in subtype A1. The number of clauses marked with " $\sharp$ " in sub-corpus CB gets to 21, of which 16 clauses are under subtype CB1, 2 clauses under CB1', another 2 under CBMC$_2$ and 1 under CBOMC$_1$. When omission occurs, the 16 clauses under subtype CB1 will surge into subtype B1. By deduction, there is great potentiality that distribution of prototypical CIPT clause patterns will skew dramatically to TSV under subtypes A1 and TV under subtype B1. This speculation is consistent with the results of an independent research conducted later on written Chinese.

• **Morphosyntactic diversity of topic markers**

One of the formal properties of CIP topics, i.e. syntactic position, is touched upon earlier in Chapter 4. Another formal property to be covered here concerns topic marker, the morphosyntactic material accompanying a topic.

Li and Thompson (1981:86) equal pause particles like "啊", "么", "呢" and "吧" to topic markers. For them, a topic can be separated from the rest of the sentence either by a pause or by a pause particle. In the present study, due to technical limitations, I have no way to give acoustic descriptions of the accurate lengths of pauses identified by ears. My discussion is thus focused on topic markers only.

Xu and Liu (1998:90) draw distinctions between elements that function exclusively as topic marker and elements that function both as topic marker and marker of other syntactic constituents. Elements of the first kind include pause particles like those mentioned by Li and Thompson that are used most often in spoken Mandarin and some others like "末", "是", etc. that are used in Shanghai dialect. Elements of the latter kind include counterparts of the construction *as for* in English that play the role of topic marker on discourse level and the role of head of an adverbial phrase on syntactic level. Prepositions like "关于" and "至于" in Chinese are elements of the latter kind and are excluded from their study. In Yuan's study （2003）, however, such distinction is ignored. Both lexical and grammatical means used to mark topics are taken into consideration. What is more, Yuan observes that lexical and grammatical means often occur together in topic structures. Constructions like "就说……吧", "你像……啊" and "所谓……呀" are examples of this sort as shown below in （22） and （23） cited from Yuan.

（22）就说咱们北京吧,有的那个话呀你没法儿写……

（23）我所谓姓查呀,不是单纯姓查……

If "就说" in （22） and "所谓" in （23） are omitted, the grammatical elements "吧" and "呀" can serve the same function.

When a content predicate functions as a topic marker, it can either precede or succeed a topic. When a compound predicate is used, it may occur in such a way that one item precedes the topic and the other succeedes it. Take for example, instances like the following （ibid）:

（24）要说咱们这个牛街确实,这个变化就是挺大的,嗯变化挺大的。

（25）小订比如说吧,男方订了这个女方的闺女了……

（26）就拿我们上班儿说吧,七点上班儿。

In （24）, the predicate "要说" goes ahead of the topic "咱们这个牛街" and is used to mark it. In （25）, the predicate "比如说" goes after the topic "小订" and is accompanied by the grammatical element "吧". In （26）, the two items of the compound predicate "就拿……说" stay apart. The latter itme is accompanied by the grammatical element "吧". In the last two cases, the grammatical element can be omitted without affecting the clause meaning.

Drawing on Li and Thompson's and Yuan's viewpoints, topic markers in the present study can be realized by either lexical or grammatical elements, or by the two combined. They are classified into three types according to the different positions they occupy. Those that occur before a topic are termed as pre-topic markers while those that occur after a topic, whether lexical or grammatical, post-topic markers. Topic markers whose first piece appears before a topic and second piece after a topic, like "就说……吧" and "就拿……说吧", are termed as circum-topic markers. Following Yuan, prepositions such as "关于" and "至于" are also included in this study. They are treated as pre-topic markers.

Fang (2002) notices that two demonstratives "这" and "那" can be used as topic markers. In the present study, "这/这个" and "那" are identified as pre-topic markers for four reasons. First, when being used to signal a topic, they always precede it. Second, they are prosodically unstressed and not used to express definite reference. Third, like other topic markers, they can be omitted from their pre-topic position without affecting the clause either syntactically or semantically. Forth, they can be accompanied by a grammatical element across the topic. To a large extent, the position of "这个" in spoken Mandarin Chinese is much less restricted than the position of other demonstratives. For the purpose of this study, "这个" is taken into account only when it occurs in the pre-topic position. To illustrate the use of the aforementioned demonstratives as pre-topic markers, consider the following examples, taken from the corpus data, in which they are marked with wavy underlining:

(27) a. 这个你这房子情况我也看了/
     b. 这个台湾有个很复杂的背景大家都知道/
     c. 那这话谁说呢/
     d. 那这一笔我想曹雪芹他不会是乱写/
     e. 这个账啊虽然是这样算/

Some other clauses taken from the corpus data are given in a separate group for comparison. In these clauses, demonstratives are used as determiners expressing definiteness and are marked with double underlining. Consider the following:

(28) a. 这个事情我不要再公开讨论/
     b. 这份委托声明书的正文部分并不是她自己亲笔写的/
     c. 这条鱼他很难拉到岸上来/

According to the recordings, each of the demonstratives in clauses (27a) ～

(27e) is unstressed and pronounced on the lowest pitch in the clause. In addition，the pronunciation of "这" and "那" somehow changes from the normal falling tone to a flat tone. In (27a)，the topic contains both a possessive pronoun "你" and a demonstrative "这" as determiners of the noun "房子". It is unnatural to treat the initial demonstrative "这个" as determiner again when the utterance is pronounced smoothly with respect to prosody and displays default stress within the tone unit. In (27b)，the topic structure is an embedded clause that expresses an event. It is signaled as a whole by "这个". In (27c) and (27d)，the topics already contain a demonstrative as a determiner. This necessitates the mere interpretation of the initial demonstratives as pre-topic markers. In (27e)，if the demonstrative，the lexical means of the compound topic marker，is omitted，the grammatical element "啊" that succeeds the topic can stand alone. This is congruous with Yuan's observation of constructions like "就说……吧" though the syntactic type of the lexical means is different. By contrast，demonstratives in clauses (28a)～(28c) are prosodically the first prominent syllable，the onset，in each tone unit though they are not the default stress. Prosodic depictions of "这个" used in different ways are obtained on the audio software Cool Edit Pro and are given below in Figure 5.3.

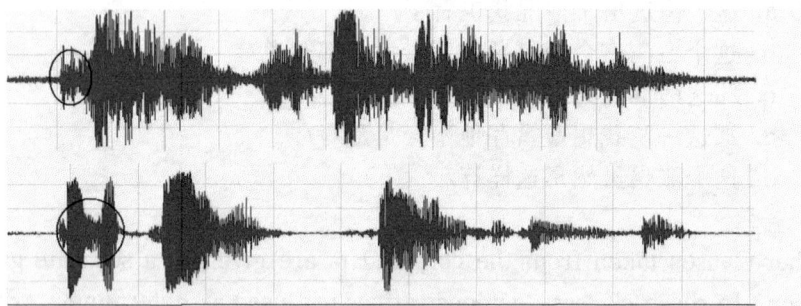

Figure 5.3　A prosodic comparison between "这个" as a pre-topic marker and as a determiner

The circled audio wave in the upper graph represents the element "这个" used in (27a) as a pre-topic marker. The circled audio wave in the lower graph indicates "这个" used in (28a) as a determiner. Their difference in wave shape shows that "这个"，in the former case，is pronounced with less stress and in a lower pitched tone in relation to the succeeding element than in the latter case. The two elements also can be distinguished by length with the former shorter in duration than the latter.

Semantically, each underlined item in the second group of clauses, when used as a determiner, confines the meaning of the noun behind so that the noun phrase as a whole refers to something mentioned prior to its current utterance or something under discussion. None of them can be omitted without affecting the clause meaning.

Whatever morphosyntactic form a topic marker takes, the common features they share lie in two aspects: first, when it is removed, neither the CIP topic nor the CIPT clause is affected; second, there is no identifiable pause between a topic marker and a topic, or the topic marker may change into a discourse marker. The investigation of different morphosyntactic means used as topic marker and their distribution in the corpus data are reported in Table 5.9 and Table 5.10 below.

Table 5.10　Morphosyntactic means of topic markers and their distribution

Morphosyntactic means	Examples	Number
Demonstrative	这	3
	那	4
	这个	8
Content predicate	比如	2
	你比如	1
	你说	2
	像	1
	就(是)	3
	所谓	2
Demonstrative + pause particle	这个……呢 这个……啊	4
Content predicate + pause particle	像……呀	1
Pause particle	呢,啊,呀	8
Pre-particle	连……	1
Preposition	至于	1

Morphosyntactic means	Examples	Number
Preposition + pause particle	至于……呢	1
N		42
%		$42/217 = 19.4$

Table 5.11 Types of topic markers and their distribution

Type	Morphosyntactic means	N_1	N_2	%
Lexical	Demonstrative	15	26	61.9
	Content predicate	11		
Lexical + grammatical	Demonstrative + pause particle	4	5	11.9
	Content predicate + pause particle	1		
Grammatical	Pause particle	8	11	26.2
	Pre-particle	1		
	Preposition	1		
	Preposition + Pause particle	1		
Total		42	42	100

As shown in Table 5.9, 42 CIPT clauses contain a topic marker, accounting for 19.4% of the corpus data. The demonstrative "这个" and pause particles "呢", "啊" and "呀" are the most frequently used means. Interestingly, although "这个" is frequent, its opposite "那个" does not occur at all. According to Table 5.10, lexical means serving the function of topic marker are of greater importance than grammatical means. The former account for 61.9 % of all the means identified, considerably surpassing the latter that account for 26.2% only. Hence the tendency for lexical means to play the role of topic marker is much stronger than that for grammatical means. This can be seen as a unique characteristic of lexical forms in Chinese. It provides good evidence for the bi-function of lexical means in the topic-prominent language. Combined means make up the smallest proportion (11.9%) of the data. Their tendency toward the role of topic marker is thus the weakest. This finding illustrates that lexical means do not rely heavily on the companionship of grammatical means to function as topic marker and that the mutual clinginess between them is loose.

5.5 A comparison between CIPT clauses in Chinese and topicalizations in English

5.5.1 TSV in Chinese vs OSV in English

CIPT clause patterns of types B and C do not have equivalents in English due to syntactic constraints. It can be assumed that their English equivalents are null sets ($\varnothing$). As far as patterns under type A are concerned, three syntactic matches are found in English irrespective of the fact that CIPT clauses are considered by some scholars basic and canonical in Chinese while topicalization constructions in English are considered derivational and non-canonical.

For the prototypical pattern TSV in Chinese, its counterpart in Englsih is OSV—a pattern most frequently mentioned in the literature. Instances of this pattern are as follows:

(29) This kind of behavior we cannot tolerate. (Radford 2002:312)

(30) Tokyo, I can't visit. (Shopen 1996:300)

(31) Jerry she can't stand. (Givon 1993b:181)

(32) This latter topic we have examined in Chapter 3 and need not reconsider.

(Quirk et al. 1985:1377)

Though having the same syntactic structure, the clauses are accounted for differently by different scholars. Radford maintains that the constituent "This kind of behavior" in (29) originates in the post-verbal position. It receives special emphasis by being moved into a more prominent position at the front of the clause, i.e. through the process of topicalization. The movement operation occurs in a way that the topicalized expression undergoes adjunction by which it is adjoined to the left of IP and leaves a trace behind in the position out of which it moves. Shopen holds that the initial proper noun "Tokyo", as shown in (30), is an external topic though it forms a core constituent and thus core argument of the transitive verb "visit". By external topic, he refers to constituents that occupy the clause-initial position but yet do not play the role of subject. When a peripheral instrument constituent like "the knife" is topicalized as in (33) below:

> (33) a. Fred sliced the bread with the knife.
>> b. With the knife Fred sliced the bread.

It is often marked with a preposition and also treated as an external topic. For Shopen, the topic is only in apposition to the clause.

With respect to (31), Givon (1993b: 181) defines it as Y-movement, or contrastive topicalization. Put differently, the formation of the construction involves fronting the contrasted element. Prosodically "Jerry" is stressed though not as strongly as the focused constituent in cleft and other contrastive-stress devices. The contextual environment Givon provides to illustrate the use of Y-movement is as follows:

> (34) a. Context: She has two brothers, Tom and Jerry.
>>   She likes Tom a lot.
>> b. Continuation:
>> i) Y-movement: ...Jerry she can't stand.
>> ii) Cleft: ...? It's Jerry that she can't stand.

The clause in (34a) establishes a context in which two members of a group are listed. They are expected to behave or be treated in a similar way. When such expectation is broken, a contrast arises. Therefore, the Y-movement construction in (34b) i) is a more appropriate continuation of the utterances in (34a) than the cleft construction in (34b) ii). In addition, Y-movement often exhibits discoursal traits of topicality. Relevant discussion in this respect will be deferred to the subsequent chapter in detail.

For Quirk et al. (1985: 1377-1378), fronting occurs in (32) in order to achieve marked theme (topic, in the present study). While providing direct linkage with what has preceded, it serves the function of arranging word order in such a way that end-focus falls on the most important part of the message. Specifically, the noun phrase "this latter topic" is moved into the initial position and the definite item "this" indicates that the marked theme expresses given information. These scholars believe that, compared to elaborate cleft and pseudocleft that are syntactically more complex, fronting, though simple in structure, is more obtrusive in terms of rhetoric.

When comparing TSV and OSV patterns, two factors have to be taken into consideration. First, while the topic in some TSV clauses may be an embedded clause or apposition construction that rarely has an equivalent in English, verb phrase topic has no English equivalent at all and is excluded from the comparison. Second, topic markers in CIPT clauses are not embodied in syntactic patterns and are also excluded from the comparison. The equivalence between TSV and OSV thus can be expressed as in (35):

(35) TSV$\longleftrightarrow$OSV (T$\neq$VP; topic marker$\notin$TSV)

It follows that the equivalence narrows down. The graph below roughly depicts this equivalence and visualizes its distribution.

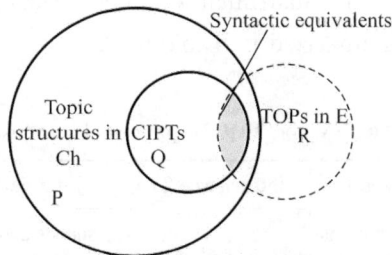

Figure 5. 4   Equivalence between CIPT clauses and TOPs

In Figure 5.4, set P stands for the collection of topic structures in Chinese, of which CIPT clauses form a portion. Set Q, forming a sub-set of P, stands for the collection of CIPT clauses. Set R represents topicalizations in English. Different types of CIPT clauses are considered as elements contained in set Q. The relationships among the sets, sub-sets and elements are expressed as follows:

(36) a. Q$\subset$P= {types A, B, CA, CB}

    b. P$\cap$R$>$Q$\cap$R

    c. Q$\cap$R= {TSV$\longleftrightarrow$OSV | T$\neq$VP; topic marker$\notin$TSV}

The intersection of sets Q and R, indicated by the grey area, contains syntactic patterns common in Chinese and English. This is where the equivalents are found. The dotted line edging the circle for topicalizations in English implies that the size cannot be assured since an accurate account of topicalization types is not available yet in the literature.

Examples of syntactic equivalents in English for two other CIPT clause patterns in Chinese are found in Radford (2002:312). They are given below:

(37) a. You know that this kind of behaviour we cannot tolerate.

b. This kind of behaviour you know that we cannot tolerate.

The patterns of (37a) and (37b) can be respectively described as MCTSV and TMCSV. In terms of their occurrence, I interviewed three native English speakers. Two of them are Americans teaching English in Shanghai Jiao Tong University. The third is an Australian engineer working in Shanghai. Their descriptions are briefly summarized in Table 5.12.

Table 5.12   Description of MCTSV and TMCSV patterns in English by native English speakers

I	Interviewee 1	Interviewee 2	Interviewee 3	II
(a) **You know** that *this kind of behavior* we cannot tolerate.	(a) sounds odd and is rarely used. Yet a' has the right word order.	(a) is less often and conventional than a'.	(a) sounds aw-kward and odd. a' seems like a complicated way of saying something fairly simple.	a' **You know** that we cannot tole-rate *this kind of behavior*.
(b) *This kind of behavior* **you know** that we cannot tolerate.	(b) is usually not used.	(b) comes even after (a).	The same as above.	b' **You know** that we cannot to-lerate *this kind of behavior*.

It is obvious from the above that structures (a) and (b) are either awkward and odd or unconventional in the eyes of the interviewees. This may be partly responsible for their rare occurrence in English.

All in all, the English equivalents of CIPT clause patterns are very limited. The most important pattern is OSV. Other patterns are infrequent or rare in use even if they are theoretically feasible.

5.5.2 Informational status of topics in TSV and OSV

Within the boundaries of a CIPT clause, normally the topic, perceived from a functional stance, is the given element. It is by no means the intonation nucleus of the tone unit that corresponds to the information unit. The new element, positioning in the comment, carries information focus and has the greatest prosodic prominence or is the intonation nucleus. There are cases, though their occurrence is quite constrained, in which the topic or part of the topic is uttered with weak stress. It is particularly so when the topicalized constituent is a demonstrative comprising one syllable, or a classifier phrase or noun phrase that contains a demonstrative as determiner. Consider:

(38) 这我也不知道/
(39) 这个要不要发/
(40) 这个钱我还是还得出的/

Prosodically, the demonstratives in the above examples are the first prominent syllable in the tone unit. "道", "发" and "还" are respectively highlighted, assigned main stress and form information climax. At this point, it is of much help to recall from Firbas (2007). Under his view of functional sentence perspective (1992: 6-7), elements contribute in different ways to the development of communication. Some contribute less by conveying information retrievable from the immediately relevant preceding context. Others contribute more by conveying information irretrievable. "The former are less dynamic than the latter". Degrees of communicative dynamism (CD) correlate with degrees of prosodic prominence (PP). His observations reveal that the distribution of non-prosodic CD matches well with that of PP. This applies to the current analysis. Information in the topic structures under examination is presented in such a linear way that the communicative value of elements increases from low to high. End-focus is hence established in accordance with placing the intonation nucleus on the final or near-final element.

As to the informational status of topics in English, understandings are divided in the literature. According to Chafe (1976:49), a clause like (41) is a contrastive one:

(41) The play, John saw yesterday.

Two foci of contrast are identified in (41). One of them is "the play", and the other is "yesterday". On the other hand, in a similar example like (42) (ibid) below:

(42) John I saw.

"John" forms a single focus of contrast. Such view is echoed to a certain extent in Givon's works. The term *contrastive topicalization* adopted by Givon (1993b: 181; 2001b: 225) invariably suggests that the construction is motivated by the contrastiveness it conveys. Put differently, the function of topicalization is to express contrast (recall example (34) above). The contrasted topic is the focused constituent though the stress accorded to it is to a lesser degree than that accorded to the fronted element in other contrastive devices such as a cleft. The viewpoint of Quirk et al. is two-angled. Fronting construction is, to them, used to achieve end-focus as well as leftward linkage as mentioned earlier. On the other hand, a more striking type of fronting, found in the language of mannered rhetoric, is often used "to point a parallelism between two parts of a clause or between two related but contrasting parts of neighboring clauses. The fronted parts may be prosodically marked as marked theme or focus, the latter typically with divided focus" (1985: 1378). Shopen (1996: 87) does not regard topic as a carrier of stress except in a contrastive construction like *speaking of Mary and Jim, Mary will like this dish, but Jim will hate it*. To Birner and Ward (1998: 36-38), the focus of a preposing construction may appear either in preposed or canonical position. Consider the following naturally occurring conversations they use to drive home this point:

(43) A: Where can I get the reading packet?
     B: In Steinberg. [Gives direction] Six dollars it costs.
(44) A: Do you watch football?
     B: Yeah. Baseball I like a lot better.

Birner and Ward argue that "Six dollars" in (43) contains the nuclear accent and serves as the focus. The preposed constituent instantiates the variable in the open proposition (= It costs X, where X is a member of the poset {prices}) and its referent is a member of the poset. In (44), which is of the same syntactic pattern as (41) by Chafe, the clause-final element "better" is the focus instead of "baseball". Briefly, "baseball" is accented not because it is the focus but because it occurs in a separate intonational phrase in clause-initial position. They argue what characterizes the preposed constituent, whether it is the focus or not, is that it serves as the link to the preceding discourse by means of a salient linking relation. As for the contrastiveness expressed by a preposed element, they hold that while Chafe's notion accounts for much of the preposing data, over half of the tokens in their own corpus (469/915, or 51%)[①] fail to satisfy his diagnostic for determining contrast (1998:40).

The example from Gregory and Michaelis (2001) cited earlier in Chapter 4 and repeated below as in (45) also reveals that topicalizations in English do not necessarily convey contrast.

(45) B: Right. [They go around in their little coaching shorts or—
    A: Right, and a T-shirt.
    B: —parachute pants]$_i$
    A: Right. That$_i$ I didn't ever understand. I mean we've got coaches...

The constituent in square parentheses is the antecedent of the demonstrative "that" in the topicalization. "That" simply denotes what has been mentioned previously in the discourse rather than form a contrast and hence expresses given information. Cases of this kind, in which the topic indicates non-contrastive prior evoking, account for 25% of their topicalization examples.

As far as topics in Chinese are concerned, Xu and Liu (1998:99) claim that compared to a contrastive focus, a topic, if it expresses a contrast, stands in

---

① It is pointed out earlier that, in Birner and Ward's (1998:31-94) study of preposing, phrasal categories that can be topicalized cover not only noun phrase, but prepositional phrase, verb phrase and adjective phrase as well. What matches the current discussion is limited to noun phrase only. Here, the percentage of 51% Birner and Ward refers to describes elements of all the four categories put together rather than noun phrase category alone. Reasonably, the percentage of the preposed noun phrases that do not carry contrast ought to be much lower than 51%.

contrast only with an entity evoked previously in the preceding discourse but is by no means the information focus within the topic structure. It is not the intonation nucleus, either. In such a structure, the focus lies somewhere in the part succeeding the topic, i.e., in the comment, instead of overlapping with the topic. My own investigation supports this viewpoint. Consider the following instance from my corpus data:

(46) 一般就是帮着他收拾收拾碗筷什么的/<u>其余的他就不让我做了</u>/

The topicalized *de* construction "其余的" in the underlined CIPT clause semantically forms a contrast with the verb phrase "收拾收拾碗筷" in the preceding clause though they belong to different syntactic categories. The verb "让" in the comment is accented and high-pitched and carries information focus. Examination of more examples of this type in the corpus leads to the same observation.

Based on such an interpretation of informational status that topics in TSV clauses enjoy and based on analysis of topicalizations in English made by Birner and Ward and Gregory and Michaelis, a comparison between the two sets of topics is tentatively depicted in Figure 5.5.

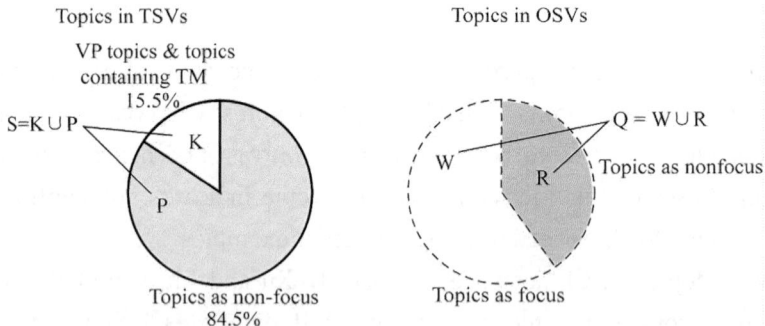

Figure 5.5 A comparison between topics in TSVs and fronted elements in OSVs

Set S contains the 71 topics from all the TSV clauses. Sub-set P stands for the collection of 60 topics as non-focus that account for 84.5% of the 71 topics. Verb phrase topics and topics that contain a topic marker amount to 11, accounting for 15.5%. Since such topics have no equivalents in OSV constructions, they are differentiated from topics in sub-set P and form sub-set K. Set Q stands for the collection of fronted elements from OSV constructions in English. It comprises sub-sets R and W. Elements in sub-set R are topics as non-focus. Elements in sub-set W are topics as contrastive focus. The dotted line separating sub-set Q from W indicates that the sizes of the two sub-sets are not assured but just estimated in that researchers are divided in this respect. The functional equivalence between non-focus topics in TSVs and their counterparts in OSVs is expressed as follows:

(47) P$\longleftrightarrow$R, P>R

The observation that sub-set P overwhelms R brings us to a quantitative comparison between the occurrence of TSV and that of OSV in the following section.

5.5.3 A quantitative comparison between TSV and OSV

Topicalizations are not rare in English although it is a subject-prominent language. Compared to CIPT clauses in Chinese, their degree of non-canonicity may be higher. This is borne out by an examination of the difference in their occurrences in the two languages. In Gregory and Michaelis (2001), 44 instances of TOP constructions are found in the informal spoken data culled from telephone conversations in English. In all, the data consists of 250,000 words. If we make a conversion of these words into minutes they will take, the comparison will be drawn more quickly. Based on the normal speaking speed at approximately 200 words per minute by native English speakers (Rossiter et al. 2006), the temporal length of Gregory and Michaelis' data is obtained in (48a). The occurrence of TOP instances per minute in their corpus is then calculated in (48b).

(48) a. $\text{Time}_E = 250,000w / 200w/m = 1250ms$
    b. Occurrence of $\text{TOP}_E = 44_i / 1250m = 0.035_i / m$
(49) a. Occurrence of all CIPT clausesC $= 217_i / 1052m = 0.206_i / m$
    b. Occurrence of TSVC $= 60_i / 1052m = 0.057_i / m$

In my own corpus where 217 instances are found, the occurrence of all CIPT clauses per minute is calculated as shown in (49a). The occurrence of TSV instances (assuming that "T$\neq$verb phrase" and "topic marker$\notin$TSV") per minute is calculated in (49b). Difference between occurrence of CIPT clauses in Chinese and that of topicalizations in English can be calculated as follows:

(50) Difference$_1$ = Occurrence of all CIPT clauses$_C$/ Occurrence of TOP$_E$
$\qquad$ = 0.206 / 0.035
$\qquad$ = 5.89

$\qquad$ Difference$_2$ = Occurrence of TSV$_C$/ Occurrence of TOP$_E$
$\qquad$ = 0.057 / 0.035
$\qquad$ = 1.63

Difference$_1$ in (50) shows that when all CIPT clauses are taken into account, their occurrence (0.206$_i$/m) is 5.89 times as much as the occurrence of TOP constructions in English (0.035$_i$/m). If the comparison is narrowed down and strictly made between CIPT clauses of TSV pattern in my own data and TOP constructions in Gregory and Michaelis' data, the occurrence of TSV pattern (0.057$_i$/m) is 1.63 times as much as that of TOP constructions, as shown by Difference$_2$. This result paves the way for the discussion of Chinese-English translations of CIPT clauses in section 5.7.

We are uncertain, however, whether or not the results apply to difference between written Chinese and English. Gregory and Michaelis observe that TOP constructions appear to be far more frequent in written English than in spontaneous spoken English. They note that they found an abundance of TOP instances in a brief search of the Brown Corpus that mainly comprises written English. A detailed knowledge of difference between written Chinese and English in this regard definitely necessitates an independent study.

5.6　An alternative perspective: a drama text-based study of CIPT clauses in written Chinese

To achieve a fuller understanding of CIPT clause patterns in Chinese, there remains another part of the task to be dealt with—CIPT clauses in written Chinese. This section is intended to probe into types and subtypes of CIPT clauses in written Chinese through text investigation and to display similarities and dissimilarities between spoken data and written data.

5.6.1 Data

The collection of written data is carried out on a small scale. The sources are confined to two Chinese dramas texts—*Teahouse* by Lao She and *Uncle Doggie's Nirvana* by Jin Yun. Drama language is treated as a source of written data in this study because it is, though reflecting spoken language to a certain extent, in essence only a simulation of speech in artificial settings, and thus makes itself a reasonable basis for the current exploration of CIPT clause patterns in written Chinese.

The data are collected from the texts following the same guidelines as followed when spoken data are collected. In all, 115 instances are obtained. They undergo the same coding processes—general and specific—as spoken data do before categorically and sub-categorically processed and statistically analyzed.

5.6.2 Syntactic patterns identified

Types and subtypes of CIPT clauses together with relevant syntactic patterns identified from the drama texts are shown in Table 5.13. Occurrences of the tokens in the corpus are presented in Table 5.14. Figure 5.6 categorically visualizes the distribution of the tokens.

Table 5.13   Types and subtypes of CIPT clauses and relevant syntactic patterns identified in *Teahouse* and *Uncle Doggie's Nirvana*

Types			Subtypes		Syntactic patterns	
A		1.	A1	1.	TSV
B		2.	B1	2.	TV
		3.	BO	3.	TVO
C	CA	4.	CA1	4.	T*shi*SV*de*
				5.	TSV*de*
	CB	5.	CB1	6.	T*shi*V*de*
		6.	CBO	7.	TVO*de*

Table 5. 14　Distribution of CIPT clauses in the written data

	A	B		CA	CB		Total
	A1	B1	BO	CA1	CB1	CBO	
N	33	70	3	5	3	1	115
		60.9	2.6		2.6	0.9	
%	28.7	63.5		4.3	3.5		100.0

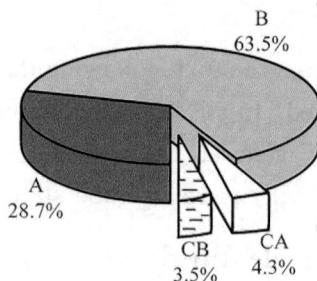

Figure 5. 6　Distribution of CIPT clauses of different types

5. 6. 3　Difference between written and spoken Chinese

According to Table 5. 13, there are only six subtypes of CIPT clauses in written Chinese. Recall from section 5. 4. 2 shows that twenty-two subtypes of CIPT clauses are identified in spoken Mandarin. Obviously, the subtypes of CIPT clauses in written Chinese are far less diverse than those in spoken Chinese. This is also true of syntactic patterns—only seven patterns are identified here while twenty-seven patterns are identified in spoken Mandarin. Table 5. 14 reveals that CIPT clauses primarily cluster under subtype B1 and secondarily under A1. They appear only sparsely in subtypes CA1 and CB1. The gap between B1 and A1 is huge. Tokens of subtype B1, standing at 60. 9% and constituting the biggest portion of the corpus data, form the prototypical and canonical subtype. TV pattern hence becomes the prototype. Unlike A1's predomination in the corpus of spoken Chinese, the frequency of A1 in the corpus of written Chinese is outnumbered by that of B1, standing at 28. 7% only. TSV pattern thus steps down from the leading prototypicality and plays second fiddle to TV pattern.

Drama language imitates authentic communication and retains some of the characteristics of naturally occurring speech. While some pragmatic features, typical of spoken language like pause, pause filler, repetition, recycling, self-repair and overlapping, etc., are either reproduced in drama language in controlled ways or deliberately not reproduced at all, elliptical syntactic structures, also typical of spoken language, tend to be reproduced to a large extent in that they are assumed to sound natural and to reduce redundancy. Not surprisingly, overimitationn of authentic communication results in the overuse of TV pattern and is responsible for its predomination in the corpus.

As for the marginality of subtypes CA1 and CB1, which respectively account for 4.3% and 2.6% of the data, one justification is that, like their counterparts in the spoken data, being sub-subtypes in the corpus in essence confines their occurrence. Besides, when the *shi...de* construction or its variations are neither a syntactic nor a semantic obligation and when their omission will not give rise to the change of clause meaning, it is preferable for them to be dropped for the sake of brevity. Put differently, their use is subject to the constraint of cognitive economy. The direct corollary of this is the low frequencies of the two subtypes and the relevant patterns under them.

Further, the use of topic markers in the written data differs a lot from that in the spoken data. According to Table 5.15 below, the types of morphosyntactic means of topic markers are extremely limited compared to those used in spoken Chinese (cf. Table 5.10 and 5.11) and are far less diverse.

Table 5.15　Morphosyntactic means of topic markers and their occurrence

Morphosyntactic means	Examples	N
Content predicate	像	1
Pre-topic particle	连……	7
Total		8
%		8/115 = 7.0

Only two forms of topic markers appear, one being a content predicate "像" and the other a pre-topic particle "连……". More importantly, topic markers occur merely 8 times here, accounting for 7.0% of the data. By contrast, topic markers occur 42 times in the spoken data, accounting for 19.4% of the data (totaling 217).

5.7　English translations of CIPT clauses

Previous discussion of informational status of topic ushers in the question of English translation of CIPT clauses. By this, I do not mean that some appropriate or good translations of CIPT clauses will be advocated here. Rather, a descriptive research on translations of CIPT clauses will be conducted and a comparison between structures of CIPT clauses and those of the translations will be made to unravel the closeness or distance between them with respect to form and function.

5.7.1　Syntax of translations

Examination of translations of CIPT clauses reveals that roughly, four kinds of structures in the target language are identified. First, the translation takes the canonical syntactic form like SVO, SVA or SVOA. In this case, the counterpart of topic is moved to the post-verbal position and plays the syntactic role of object of verb, or moved to post-prepositional position, also the clause-final position and plays the syntactic role of object of preposition. Second, the original is translated in such a way that the translation bears no syntacto-semantic correspondence to the original. Yet the counterpart of the topic occupies the clause-initial position or a near-clause-initial position and precedes the counterpart of the original comment. Third, the translation is a passive and the topic is translated as the syntactic subject, occupying the clause-initial position. Forth, the translation is a non-canonical topicalization construction, i. e. OSV, and the counterpart of the topic occupies the clause-initial position, grammatically serving as the object of verb. Examples below are illustrations of the syntactic forms that a translation may take. For this purpose, examples are taken from the English versions of the drama texts mentioned earlier as well as from the English versions of two other written texts—*The Family* by Ba Jin (translated by Ying Ruocheng and published in 1999) and *Fortress Besieged* by Qian Zhongshu (translated by Kelly and Mao and published in 2003). The original is given in (a) and the English translation in (b).

- **Topic translated as object of verb in SVO**

SVO is the most frequently adopted syntactic construction in translating CIPT clauses. Consider:

(51) a. 他是死是活，我不知道。

    b. I don't know whether he is alive or dead.   (*Teahouse* Act Ⅱ)

(52) a. ……这钱我可不能领。

    b. ...but I can't accept the money.   (*Fortress Besieged* Chapter 4)

(53) a. ……黄花闺女都能娶……

    b. ...you could marry a virgin...   (*Uncle Doggie's Nirvara* Scene 5)

Both (51a) and (52a) are of TSV pattern. The topic of (51a) is translated as an objective clause in (51b) while the topic in (52a) is translated as the object of the predicate verb "accept". (53a) is a TV clause, in which the agent argument of the predicate verb "娶" is understood but syntactically unexpressed. In (53b), the agent argument is added according to the context. The counterpart of the topic is placed in the post-verbal position, playing the grammatical role of object. The canonical, unmarked SVO construction is adopted in all the three translations alike. The same translation applies even when the topic occurs initially within an embedded CIPT clause：

(54) a. ……我老觉得我的话你懂。   (*The Family* Scene 3, Act Ⅱ)

    b. ...I always felt you would understand what I mean.

The clause pattern of (54a) is MCTSV. In (54b), the counterpart of the topic is moved to the post-verbal position in the embedded clause. The translation thus is in the form of MCSVO.

- **Topic translated as object of preposition in SVOA / SVA**

Conforming to the principle of end-weight, a topic in Chinese may be translated into the target language as object of preposition that occupies the clause-final position. Consider：

(55) a. 太爷爷俺没听说过……   (*Uncle Doggie's Nirvara* Scene 14)

    b. I never learnt anything about my great-grandfather.

(56) a. ……谎是撒不得的。   (*Fortress Besieged* Chapter 6)

    b. ...you can't get away with a lie.

(57) a. ……前一次我带你出去看现代剧的事，不知谁告诉三爸了。

                       (*The Family* Scene 1, Act Ⅱ)

b. . . . somebody told Third Uncle about my taking you to that performance of modern plays.

Instance (55a) is a TSV clause. The structure of its translation in (55b) is SVOA, an unmarked syntactic pattern in English. The topic "太爷爷" is translated as the object of the preposition "about". (56a) is a type C topic structure in which the *shi . . . de* construction is used. The agent of the verb "撒" is syntactically unexpressed. The translation is of SVA form in which the agent is added and the original topic is translated as the object of the preposition "with". The syntactic pattern of (57a) is TMCSVO. The CIPT clause contains an embedded topic structure that constitutes the internal argument of the matrix verb "知". The verb "告诉" is semantically trivalent, denoting a relation among three entities. Since the topic is a noun phrase of length and complexity that contains a relative clause, its counterpart is positioned clause-finally in (57b), forming the object of the preposition "about", or put differently, functioning as peripheral argument (Shopen 1996:301) introduced by the preposition "about". The end-weight principle is therefore observed in the translation such that the part following the verb is longer and heavier than the part that precedes the verb (cf. Quirk et al. 1985:1040). The matrix clause "不知" is excluded in the translation and (57b) takes the form of SVOA.

- **Original syntacto-semantic relation not retained**

The syntacto-semantic relation in the original is not always retained in the translation. Consider:

(58) a. 现大洋不容易看到啊！ (*Teahouse* Act Ⅲ)

b. Silver dollars are hard to come by.

(59) a. 打女学生的钱,我不要。 (ibid)

b. Money earned by beating girl students? I don't want it.

Example (58a) is a TV clause in which the topic "现大洋" is retrievable from the previous discourse and is coreferential with the gap succeeding the verb "看到". The actor of the verb "看到" is dropped. The syntax of (58b) differs from that of the original. Yet "silver dollar", the counterpart of the topic, occurs in the initial position for given information and well matches the original topic with respect to

100

its informational status. The translation of (59a) consists of two clauses. The topicalized noun phrase "打女学生的钱" in the original is translated as an elliptical question. The original comment is translated as an SVO construction in which "it" is added as a grammatical object and anaphorically refers to the entity "money" in the preceding clause. The two clauses are thus coherently connected by means of this cohesive tie. What characterizes the translations in these two cases is that the counterpart of the topic is retained in the clause-initial position. Admittedly, such a word order corresponds to the original better than if the counterpart is moved rightward to the post-verbal position because it reflects the situation to a full extent that what is expressed in the original is uppermost in the speaker's mind.

- **Topic structure translated as a passive**

  Sometimes a CIPT clause is translated as a passive. Consider the following:

  (60) a. 这脸只有小时候母亲亲过……   (*The Family* Scene 1, Act Ⅱ)

      b. As a baby, my cheeks have been kissed by my mother.

  (61) a. ……鬃也不打,毛也不梳-   (*Uncle Doggie's Nirvara* Scene 9)

      b. …the mane is not combed, the hair not brushed—

A passive construction is employed in (60b) and the counterpart of the topic "这脸" crops up near-clause-initially as the grammatical subject while the agent is translated as a by-phrase element. Though syntactically marked, the translation presents familiar information before unfamiliar information. Instance (61a) contains two topic structures in coordination. Both are translated as passives in coordination. The counterparts of the original topics are treated as definite expressions denoting given information, occupying the clause-initial positions.

- **Topic translated as fronted element in OSV**

  Occasionally, CIPT clauses are transformed into OSV constructions. Consider:

  (62) a. 我跟他的关系,我也忘了。   (*Fortress Besieged* Chapter 7)

      b. My relationship with him—I've forgotten myself.

  (63) a. ……没的能有……   (*Uncle Doggie's Nirvara* Scene 10)

      b. …what you don't have you will have.

The word order in examples （62b） and （63b） exactly corresponds to that in the original. Yet since OSV construction is considered marked and non-canonical in English in which the principle of end-focus is stuck to, its occurrence is rare in translation.

5.7.2　An empirical study of CIPT clause translations

This part is intended to obtain an empirical understanding of the syntactic structures used in CIPT clause translations. Three steps are taken to achieve such a goal. First, translations of CIPT clauses are collected. Second, a statistical analysis is made. Third, results are reported and discussed.

5.7.2.1　Data

The sources of data are confined to the English version of the two drama texts （*Teahouse and Uncle Doggie's Nirvana*） in the hope that the translation study forms an extension of the previous section. The former drama text is translated by John Howard-Gibbon and the latter by Ying Ruocheng. Translations of the 115 tokens in the written data are collected from the texts. They are put into four different groups, I, II, III and IV, on the basis of the syntactic structure they take and on the basis of where the counterpart of a topic is placed in the structure. The groups of the structures and the types of CIPT clauses are then arranged in a table such that a variable of one series is presented in relation to a variable of the other series.

5.7.2.2　Results

Statistical investigation into syntactic structures used in CIPT clauses translations yields the results as follows.

According to Table 5.16, the canonical SVO structure, in which the counterpart of topic plays the grammatical role of object of verb, predominates to such an extent that it occurs 60 times, accounting for 52.2% of the 115 CIPT clause translations. If we take into consideration those structures in which topics are translated as the object of preposition, the tendency to move the counterpart of CIP topic rightward in the TL is overwhelming though it proves the claim by Shao and Zhao （2003） and Shao and Yu （2006） to be simplistic that the translations of CIPT clauses, as a rule, take the syntactic form of SVO. The occurrence of liberal translations of which the structure bears no syntacto-semantic correspondence with the original is significant and comes second, accounting for 21.7%. Passives are used infrequently and occur 9 times. OSV is marginal in the target language, occurring only 4 times. It is demonstrated in section 5.5.3 that the occurrence of CIPT clauses in spoken Mandarin is 5.89 times as much as that of OSV clauses in spoken English per minute while the occurrence of TSV clauses is 1.63 times as much as that of OSV clauses. When examining the difference between the occurrence of CIPT clauses of all types in written Chinese and the occurrence of OSV clauses in their English translations, the gap, as shown in calculation (64a), stands at 28.75 times.

Table 5.16 Distribution of syntactic structures in the data of translations

	I			II	III		IV					
	Counterpart of topic moved rightward in translation			No syntacto-semantic correspondence betw. SL and TL	Passive		OSV		No counterpart for topic*		Total	
	As object of v		As object of prep										
	N	%	N	%	N	%	N	%	N	%	N	%	N	%
A	17	14.8	7	6.1	6	5.2	0	0.0	2	1.7	1	0.9	33	28.7
B	37	32.2	7	6.1	17	14.8	8	7.0	2	1.7	2	1.7	73	63.5
CA	4	3.5	0	0.0	1	0.9	0	0.0	0	0.0	0	0.0	5	4.3
CB	2	1.7	0	0.0	1	0.9	1	0.9	0	0.0	0	0.0	4	3.5
Pooled	60	52.2	14	12.2	25	21.7	9	7.8	4	3.5	3	2.6	115	100.0

* Note: Out of the original 115 CIPT clauses in the corpus, three are translated in a way that the topics have no counterpart in the target language.

(64) a. Difference$_1$ = 115/4 = 28.75

b. Difference$_2$ = 33/4 = 8.25

The difference between the occurrence of TSV clauses and that of OSV translations is 8.25 times as shown in (64b). If we roughly compare the two pairs of figures (5.89 vs 28.75 and 1.63 vs 8.25), it is obvious that the OSV construction is considerably underused in the target language.

5.7.3　Gap between SL and TL

5.7.3.1　Topic as non-focus vs object as focus

Clause topics in Chinese are psychologically based (Pan 1997: 265), embodying what is uppermost in the mind of the speaker or writer. Xu and Liu (1998:99) point out that the focus in a topic structure falls on a certain element in the comment rather than on the topic. The topic is not the focus or marked focus at any rate. This holds good even when the structure is a contrastive one. On the other hand, however, the word order of SVO in English is an unmarked structure where "O" carries the focus. In this sense, when a CIPT clause is translated as SVO, the informational status of "O" in the TL does not match that of the topic in the SL though "O" plays the same semantic role as the original topic does. When a topic is translated as object of preposition that occupies the clause-final position and forms the carrier of focus, the object does not match the original topic, either, with respect to their difference in informational status.

According to communicative dynamism (CD) (Firbas 2007:105), the position an element occupies is related to the progression of communication. The more the element occurs near the completion of this progression, the more its informational value or importance. On average, the informational value of elements exhibits an ascending tendency with their positions changing from left to right in a clause. When "O" in the TL is followed by other elements and hence does not occupy the final position as exemplified in (65b) below:

(65) a. 这样丑的老婆,在中国也娶得到…… (*Fortress Besieged* Chapter 6)
　　b. You can find such an ugly wife in China, too.

the final element, "too" in case, carries the focus. It has high informational value in the information unit of this clause from the perspective of CD. The information value of the adverbial phrase "in China" is comparatively lower. As for the object noun phrase "such an ugly wife" that stands at medium in the translation, its information value is even lower than that of the two elements on its right, but yet is not the lowest anyhow. It is still higher than that of the elements on its left. This is quite different from the case in (65a) where the initial unit "这样丑的老

婆" is obviously given. Accordingly, the informational status of the object in the TL does not reflect that of the topic in the SL.

When translations take the form of a passive, the syntactic subject represents information either given (discourse-old) or shared (hearer-old). This is congruent with Birner and Ward's (1998:200) observation that "the subject NP in a by-phrase passive must not represent less familiar information within the discourse than does the NP within the by-phrase". In this sense, a passive translation matches the original better though it differs from it as a syntactically marked construction. Presumably, it is on this ground that Liu (2006:333) argues that TR (theme-rheme) clauses have an extensive potential to be translated as passives. When a translation is a syntacto-semantically non-corresponding construction, the counterpart of topic is often positioned clause-initially, represents given or familiar information and matches the original to a larger extent with respect to informational status.

5.7.3.2 Realization of discoursal property

One of the properties the topic possesses is that it fulfills discourse function. Namely, the topic represents an entity already mentioned in the preceding discourse (Tsao 1977/ 1995:92-99; Shi 2000). Similarly, Gregory and Michaelis (2001) prove that in English, the great majority of the denotata of the preclausal NPs in TOP are anaphoric for being a member of an activated set or previously mentioned. Such views are empirically collaborated and developed in chapter 6 of the present study. For the time being, we simply give a passing reference to discourse property inherent in CIP topics in order to illustrate the mismatch or non-equivalence between CIPT clauses and their usual translations when the counterpart of a topic is placed in the canonical post-verbal or clause-final position. Consider the following in which the CIPT clause is underlined:

(66) a. ⋯⋯咱们的茶馆改了良,<u>你的小辫儿也该剪了吧?</u> (*Teahouse* Act II)

    b. Our teahouse has put on a new face; shouldn't you cut off your old queue?

In the original, through the pair of possessive pronouns "咱们的" and "你的", the CIP topic "你的小辫儿" forms a contrast with the expression "咱们的茶馆" in the preceding clause and is cohesively connected with it. The predicate "剪" is the intonation nucleus and carrier of focus. In the translation, however, the counterpart of the topic is moved to the clause-final position though the semantic structure of the original remains unchanged. The unit "your old queue" forms the focus where the intonation nucleus lies. Apparently, "new" and "old" stand in contrast but they do not in essence in that the indefinite noun phrase "a new face" does not expresses reference at all while "your old queue" has a definite reference. The original contrast hence loses itself in the TL.

Sometimes discoursal association realized by a CIP topic is weakened when SVO translation is adopted in the TL. Consider as an example:

(67) (狗儿爷:好嘛,又要<u>割尾巴</u>－儿媳妇你先避一避,我让大伙儿瞧瞧,看咱狗儿爷腚上有尾巴没有?

祁小梦:(款款地)万江大叔,老人正病着,别惊动他了。这风水坡上<u>犯了什么法,犯了什么罪</u>,我姓祁的顶着,我跟你们走,走吧。

狗儿爷:闺女,你走了,谁还给俺送饭哪?

[冯金花出现在人群当中]

冯金花:李万江,当初我跟你怎么说的? 你又是怎么应的? 你喝了迷魂汤似的要干什么? 你那个小乌纱帽儿值几个钱? 不顶吃,不顶喝,还那么贪着它,二郎爷喝西北风——你有这神瘾? 不干正好,少昧良心。)

a. <u>这割尾巴的官司我打了</u>,天大的事朝我说……

(*Uncle Doggie's Nirvana* Scene 12)

b. I'll take care of this 'cutting tails' business. Let them come to me.

In (67), the part in brackets is the discourse chunk preceding the CIPT clause. The underlined topic structure in (67a) is of TSV pattern. The verb phrase "割尾巴" contained in the topicalized item occurs previously in the chunk. It is a lexical repetition in the current CIPT clause and, based on Halliday and Hasan (1976), forms a cohesive tie with its antecedent. The head noun of the topic "官司" stands in a semantic relation with "犯了什么法" and "犯了什么罪" if the items are treated as members of a set pertinent to law. The demonstrative determiner "这" denotes what has already been mentioned in the prior discourse. The noun phrase in TOP as a whole is cohesively associated with what has been talked about earlier and draws in new information in the comment. Admittedly, the topic's occupation

106

of clause-initial position allows it to be formally in the proximity of what it is semantically related to. Such syntactic positioning is in line with iconic proximity (Ungerer and Schmid 2001; Zhao 2000:160) and is instrumental in information processing. Moreover, it is conducive to building up specific-general connection between the topic of the current CIPT clause and the topic—"天大的事" of the succeeding CIPT clause. Instance (67b) shows that "this 'cutting tails' business", the counterpart of the topic under discussrion, is a long and heavy element. It is hence placed in the post-verbal position. In the same way as the topic does in the original, the counterpart item plays the semantic role of patient and is governed by the verb phrase "take care of". Yet, it differs from the topic in two ways. First, it constitutes the focus in the TL with "business" being stressed whereas the topic is given in the SL. Second, occupying the clause-final position, the item hardly embodies the cognitive principle of iconic proximity as far as its antecedents are concerned. The extent to which it contributes to the establishment of anaphoric association is thus quite limited.

Things may be different when a CIPT clause is translated as a non-SVO construction. For example, in a discourse chunk such as the following:

(68) a. 姑娘，说话留点神！ <u>一句话说错了</u>，什么都可以变成逆产！

(Teahouse Act Ⅲ)

    b. You must be careful what you say, Miss. One wrong word can turn anything into "traitor's property".

The item "一句话" in TOP in the underlined topic structure has an indefinite reference. It stands in a complex lexical repetition (cf. Hoey 1991) relation with "说话" in the preceding clause and serves the discourse function of anaphoric association. As far as semantic structure is concerned, the translation in (68b) does not match the original at all for the whole topic structure is converted into a subject noun phrase "one wrong word". However, the discourse property realized by the topic in the original is retained thanks to the placement of its counterpart noun phrase in the clause-initial position. The head of the noun phrase "word" bears a collocation relation to the verb "say" in the preceding clause. Coherence between them is thus intensified with the two elements being formally proximate. When a passive is used in a translation, the counterpart of a CIP topic normally plays the grammatical role of subject and occupies the clause-initial position. Discourse property of the topic will be retained likewise. In such a case, the translation plausibly matches the original better than an unmarked SVO translation does as far as informational status and discoursal association are concerned.

5.8 Summary

In this chapter, attention is focused on the syntax of CIPT clauses. The data are typed and subtyped. Altogether, twenty-seven syntactic patterns are identified and their distribution in the corpus is explored. TSV and TV are found to be the most prototypical patterns in terms of their frequencies. Topic markers are diverse in their morphosyntactic forms. They come under 3 types: lexical, lexical and grammatical and grammatical. Quite beyond the usual expectation, lexical topic markers predominate in the data. A comparison is made between TSV clauses in Chinese and topicalizations in English drawing on analyses of topicalizations provided mainly in Birner and Ward (1998) and Gregory and Michaelis (2001). Investigation reveals that the occurrence of TSV clauses per minute in my own corpus data is found to be 1.63 times as much as that of topicalizations in Gregory and Michaelis'.

An independent research is conducted on written Chinese based on data collected from two drama texts. The results show that, different from what is revealed in the spoken data, CIPT clause patterns are far less diverse in the written data. Besides, TV pattern far outnumbers TSV pattern and forms the prototype. The chapter carries out an empirical investigation of the syntactic constructions adopted in the English translations of the written data. SVO is found to be most frequently used. Paradoxically, viewed from perspectives of informational structure and discoursal association, the construction is by no means the most appropriate. On the contrary, some important traits of equivalence do exist between an infrequent translations and the original.

Chapter 6   CIP topics:
discoursal associations

6.1   Introduction

It is briefly noted in the previous chapter that a CIP topic fulfills the discourse function of connecting with an entity either in the preceding or in the subsequent discourse, or with entities in both the preceding and succeeding discourse. Such links are termed discoursal associations in this study. They are differentiated on account of their different directions in a discourse chunk in relation to the topic in question. The ones that designate leftward links are leftward associations. Those that designate rightward links are rightward associations. The associations are similar to what Givon (1983; 1995a; 1995b:78) describes as referential distance and topic persistence. In this chapter a corpus-based research is conducted on how discoursal associations on the part of CIP topics are established and how they distribute. Section 6.2 presents research questions. Section 6.3 explains how discoursal associations are established by means of semantic connections and how they are measured. Sections 6.4 and 6.5 form the heart of this chapter. Section 6.4 presents how semantic connections between topics or elements contained in them and constituents in contextual clauses are identified. It presents data analysis as well. In section 6.5, research results are presented. Patterns of associations are hence revealed. Section 6.6 provides a cognitive interpretation of discoursal associations on the part of CIP topics. In addition, it presents differences in discoursal associations between CIP topics in Chinese and topicalized items in English. Finally, Section 6.7 presents a summary.

6.2   Research questions

The questions this chapter intends to address include:
1) How are CIP topics or elements contained in them semantically connected

with constituents in contextual clauses within the scope of discourse chunk?

2) What discoursal association patterns do CIP topics exhibit through establishing semantic connections?

3) In what ways are the association patterns of CIP topics in Chinese different from those of the preclausal NPs in TOP in English?

Question 1) in fact has to do with identification of semantic relations that hold between a topic or an element embedded in a topic and a relevant constituent in a contextual clause. Question 2) further comprises two sub-questions: a) How are discoursal associations measured? b) How do they distribute in the corpus data? Concerning question 3), I will again avail myself of Gregory and Michaelis's (2001) research for the English part. A comparison is thus to be made between discourse function of CIP topics in Chinese and that of topicalized NPs in English based on my own research on the former and theirs on the latter.

6.3　Measurements of discoursal associations

6.3.1　Size of discourse chunk

Givon (1983:7-8) holds that when a thematic paragraph is viewed as a unit comprising strings of clauses, admittedly, it involves factors that serve to establish a mechanism operating at different levels while simultaneously realizing discourse and syntax. Such factors can be described as thematic continuity, action continuity and topic/participant continuity. Of the three, topic/participant continuity forms the main focus in the study of thematic paragraph. To obtain measures of this continuity, Givon sets the arbitrary upper bound of clauses to the left of the measured topic at the value of 20. As for the number of clauses to the right, the minimal value recorded is "0". No value is set as maximal such that "the topic/ participant continues an uninterrupted presence as a semantic argument of the clause, an argument of whatever role and marked by whatever grammatical means" (ibid:15). Later, when the same scholar changes the original notion of "topic continuity" to "topicality" (1993b; 1995a; 1995b), referential distance of a referent is measured within the range of 3 clauses to the left of the referent and topic persistence is measured within the range of 10 clauses to the right of the referent (1995b: 79). Gregory and Michaelis (2001) question such an extent of examination. They hold that "looking 10 clauses ahead generally provided no more insight into the discourse status of the prclauseal-NP denotattum than did looking at only 5 subsequent utterances". In their own research, 5 clauses following the measured topic are examined when the discourse status of the preclausal-NP denotatum is under scrutiny. In the present study, my concern is how CIP topics are discoursally associated in spoken Chinese but not how far the associations can extend. For this purpose, an examination of the adjacent discourse of a topic structure is believed to be more practical than that of a whole thematic paragraph. Drawing on relevant ideas by the researchers mentioned above but yet with modifications, the size of a discourse chunk is therefore set at 9 clauses. Namely, 4 continuous contextual clauses stand both to the left and right of a CIPT clause. These clauses together with a CIPT clause form a discourse chunk. Within this scope, semantic connections through which discoursal associations on the part of the topics are established will be probed into.

6.3.2   Semantic connection

Semantic connection refers to the relation holding between a topic or an element contained in a topic and a constituent in a contextual clause. Semantically, it is realised as various bonds like lexical reiteration, collocation, co-reference, preview-detail, etc. The connection resembles cohesion to a large extent. Yet, in this study, it is exclusively confined to the two members of a pair, one being unexceptionally a topic or an element contained in a topic, the other an item in a contextual clause. Viewing from the angle of the CIPT clause, semantic connections extend in two ways: leftward and rightward. They provide the means for investigating discoursal associations. Specifically, leftward semantic connections embody leftward associations while rightward semantic connections embody rightward ones.

6.3.3   Gauging of discoursal associations

Since the examination of discoursal associations is confined within the scope of discourse chunk, their measurements are naturally carried out within the same scope. As already stated, a chunk contains one target clause—the CIPT clause embracing a CIP topic—plus eight contextual clauses. The CIPT clause stands in the middle of a chunk with four clauses occurring before it and four after it. All the clauses except the CIPT clause are called contextual clauses. They are differentiated according to their different positions in the chunk and are correspondingly so coded. The four clauses standing to the left of the CIPT clause occupy four positions ranging from 4 to 1. These positions, from left to right, are coded respectively as left 4, left 3, left 2 and left 1. Namely, position left 4 is the leftmost or farthest away from the CIPT clause and position left 1 is the nearest to the CIPT clause. Positions left 2 and left 3 are in between, the former being the second from the CIPT clause and the latter the third from it. The clauses occupying these positions are recorded correspondingly as L4, L3, L2 and L1. Contextual clauses standing to the right of the CIPT clause are coded in the reserve order. From left to right, the positions the four contextual clauses occupy range from 1 to 4. The position that succeeds the CIPT clause immediately is coded right 1. It is the nearest to the CIPT clause. Position right 4 is the rightmost and farthest away from the CIPT clause. In the same way, right 2 and right 3 are in between them. The clauses in these positions are correspondingly recorded as R1, R2, R3 and R4. The diagram below can give an explicit and visual representation of the structure of a discourse chunk.

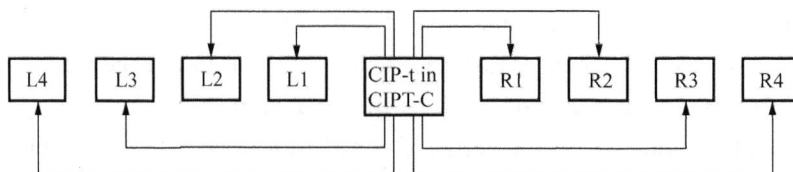

| L4 | L3 | L2 | L1 | CIP-t in CIPT-C | R1 | R2 | R3 | R4 |

Figure 6.1   Structure of a discourse chunk

Each of the arrow lines points from the CIPT clause to one of the contextual clauses. It signals how the associations on the part of the CIP topic in a CIPT clause with the contextual clauses are checked. The measurements of the associations bear some resemblance to the discourse measurements of topic continuity or topicality proposed by Givon (1983; 1995a; 1995b:78-79). If a CIP topic or an element in such a topic semantically relates to an element in a certain contextual clause or to a certain complete contextual clause as a demonstrative CIP topic may do, a value will be assigned. To measure its discoursal associations in different positions, value "1", "2", "3" or "4" will be assigned respectively. Therefore, each value reflects the position in which a related contextual clause stands. This also applies to cases where the related element is a zero form. The slot is then represented by Ø[①]. In the process of value assignment, the semantic role the related element plays in the contextual clause is ignored. Further, the grammatical function that the related element serves is ignored as well. Suppose a CIP topic or an element contained in it bears no semantic relationship to any element in a certain contextual clause, the symbol "x"[②], standing for "no connection", will be assigned to the position of that clause. The following example is an illustration.

(1) L4 他本来站在车上/L3 或者步兵穿*裙子*也没关系/L2 那现在骑马了/L1 穿*裙子*怎么骑法呢/所以<u>服装要改革</u>/R1 不但要学匈奴人骑射的*服装*/R2 而且*服装*本身要紧身/R3 Ø 要能够符合战争的需要/R4 那么所以他就提出来要进行*服饰*的改革/

In (1), the bare noun topic "服装" in the underlined CIPT clause semantically relates to the underlined noun phrase "裙子" in clauses L3 and L1. The semantic relation between "裙子" and "服装" can be described as specific-general or hyponym-superordinate. Values "3" and "1" are respectively assigned to the two clauses. Concerning clauses L2 and L4, no semantic relationship of any type is identified between the topic and any element in them. The symbol "x" is thus assigned to both clauses. When examining the topic's semantic relation with the right-ward subsequent discourse, we see clearly that the phrase in TOP, "服装", is repeated in clauses R1 and R3 though "服装" in these three clauses has different referents. The initial zero form in R3 refers anaphorically to "服装" in clause R2 and is indirectly associated with the topic. Finally the topic is paraphrased as "服

---

① Throughout this section, a zero form is interpreted as standing for what is unexpressed. Its antecedent is recoverable from the preceding discourse. It is roughly the same as ellipsis, particularly nominal ellipsis. In Halliday and Hasan (1976:142-166), ellipsis is regarded as substitution by zero and serves as a grammatical means of cohesion. In the present study, the anaphoric function that a zero form fulfils in discourse is emphasized for the purpose of investigating discoursal associations of CIP topics. Accordingly, a slot embodied by "Ø" is always treated as marking discoursal association whether it co-refers with the head of a noun phrase or with a whole noun phrase.

② The reason that the symbol "x" instead of value "0" is used resides in the fact that "0" is counted as a valid value in the Excel system when statistic analysis is made in a latter stage. Thus "x" can avoid miscomputation.

饰" in R4. "服饰" can also be viewed as a near synonym of "服装" and thus interpreted as semantically related to the topic regardless of the fact that the grammatical function it serves in R4 differs from that the topic serves in the CIPT clause. Values "1", "2", "3" and "4" are respectively assigned to the four rightward clauses. The recording of the semantic relations identified in example (1) and the assigning of values are shown in the diagram below：

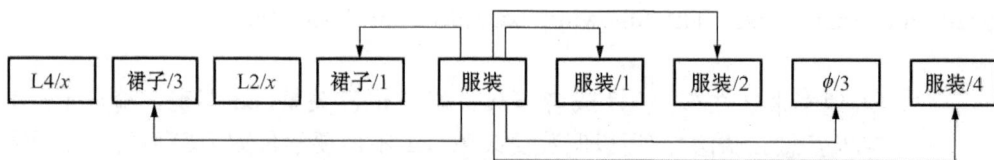

| L4/x | 裙子/3 | L2/x | 裙子/1 | 服装 | 服装/1 | 服装/2 | φ/3 | 服装/4 |

Figure 6. 2　Coding of semantic relations and value assignment：Example (1)

In Figure 6.2，all the connected items found in the contextual clauses are picked out and listed. Arrow lines are drawn from the box signifying the CIP topic to boxes signifying the contextual clauses in different positions that contain the items related to the topic. The values assigned designate both semantic relatedness and positions of the related items. The symbol "x" designates non-relatedness. The clause that contains an "x" bears no arrow line. Consider another example：

（2）B：……就是应该教书/L4 把学生教好/L3 这是你的天职/
　　　A：L2 当时您也这么想/
　　　B：L1 我也是这样想/其实那<u>一二一游行</u>很多学生都去参加了/R1 我就没去参加 Ø①/我就是在……R2 因为它经过我住的那个房子那条路游行/R3 我就在那旁边看 Ø/R4 但我没参加 Ø/

In example（2），the CIP topic "一二一游行" has no left-ward semantic relation. To the right of the CIPT clause，the zero form in contextual clauses R1，R3 and R4 are all coreferential with the topic. Values "1"，"3" and "4" are thus assigned to these clauses. The pronominal "它" in clause R2 anaphorically refers back to the

---

① There are two other potential positions the zero form may occupy in this clause，one being the initial，another between the subject and the predicate. Since "参加" is a two-place predicate，the zero form is assumed to occupy the post-verbal position here on account of the semantic role it plays.

CIP topic. The verb "游行" in the same clause morphologically repeats part of the topic—the head of the topical noun phrase—but differs in grammatical function. Yet，clause R2 still receives value "2" though it contains two elements semantically relating to the topic. A diagrammatic representation of example (2) is drawn as follows.

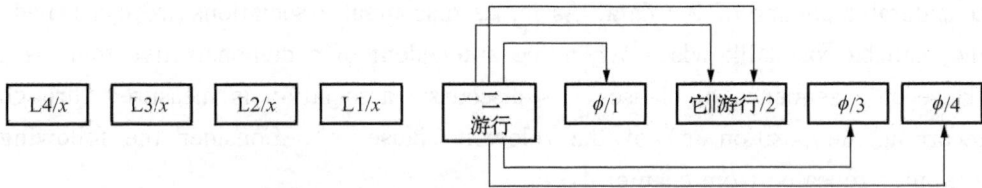

Figure 6.3 Coding of semantic relations and value assignment：Example (2)

Here in Figure 6.3，the topic has no left-ward association and "x" is assigned to all the contextual clauses to the left of the CIPT clause. It follows that no arrow line directs towards the left. By contrast，all the contextual clauses to the right of the CIPT clause are pointed to by arrow lines drawn from the box occupying the middle position in the discourse chunk. This means that all the elements listed in the rightward boxes are semantically related to the CIP topic. Two arrow lines are drawn towards clause R2 but yet the assignment of value "2" is not affected.

When a chunk is part of a conversation，which is normally characterized by changes of speakers' turns，it's very likely that the CIPT clause and the contextual clauses occur in different turns. Nevertheless，the rules for value assignment remain the same. Consider：

(3) B：……L4(嘉峪关)修起来了以后/L3 余了一块砖/
　　A：L2 只多了一块砖/
　　B：L1 多了一块砖/这块砖多出来了以后呢/R1 这个官吏就刁难他/R2 找
　　　　他的事/R3 说你不是说 Ø 绝无余缺吗/R4 为什么多出来一块 Ø/

In this example，the topicalized noun phrase "这块砖" has both leftward and rightward semantic connections. To the left，it co-refers with the noun phrase "一块砖" in the adjacent clause L1 and in clauses L2 and L3 across turns. Its head "砖" repeats the head of the phrase "一块砖". Values "1"，"2" and "3" are assigned to L1, L2 and L3. As for the right-ward clauses, the head of the topic "砖" is anaphorically referred to by zero form in R3 and R4. Admittedly, the topic relates to clauses R3 and R4 and values "3" and "4" are assigned. All the other contextual clauses in which no element bears any semantic relation with the topic receives "x" in coding.

It is noted in Chapter 4 that demonstratives functioning as CIP topics form a considerable portion of the data. As far as discoursal associations are concerned, they can be coded likewise. When the antecedent of a demonstrative topic is a clause or a sequence of clauses, its discoursal association is measured through recording the position (s) of the relevant clause (s). Consider the following example, repeated from chapter 4:

(4) L4 *所以在那三年中得到那么多文化界的保护这样走过来了*/L3 *所以走的时候呢*/L2 *文化界想要留我的那个力量非常非常大*/L1 *所以走得非常非常地困难*/<u>那个</u>是在开始时候没有想到的/R1 那因此说就是说那么为什么如此地坚决还是走/R2 还是离开/R3 主要的原因可能是觉得那个三年之中我自己心里抱着这个打算就是打那个基础/R4 好像是你要建个非常大的楼……

The topicalized demonstrative "那个" refers anaphorically back to clauses L3, L2 and L1, that can be seen as, in Quirk et al.'s terms (1985:375), 'sentential antecedents'. The nature of anaphoric demonstrative, through which semantic relatedness is achieved, is not agreed on, though, by different scholars. It falls within grammatical means of textual cohesion in Halliday and Hasan (1976). The same phenomenon is captured in Hoey's (1991:72) study of lexical repetition. Following Hoey's view, demonstrative pronouns used anaphorically are treated in the present study as a lexical means marking semantic connections on the part of CIP topics. Accordingly, values designating such connections in example (4) are recorded respectively as "3", "2" and "1". Other clauses in the chunk, bearing no relation with the topic, are therefore recorded as "x". The same is true with a topic that contains a demonstrative determiner. Consider:

(5) L4 *所以贾家呢小说里边呢是有一个王妃的*/L3 *因此探春在抽到这个签*/L2 *大家为什么跟她说*ⱽ *我们家已经有了一个王妃啊*/L1 *难道你也要成为王妃吗*/<u>这个话</u>实际上是生活当中曹家人当时说过的话/R1 曹雪芹就把它写进

去了/R2 明白吧/R3 他写 Ø 这个时候呢/R4 因为他还没有统稿……

"这个" in the underlined CIPT clause occurs as a determiner and the noun phrase in TOP "这个话" has as its antecedent both the embedded clause "我们家已经有了一个王妃" in clause L2 and "难道你也要成为王妃吗" as a whole. Clause L1 receives value "1" and L2 "2". For the subsequent discourse，"这个话" in turn becomes the antecedent of the pronominal constituent "它" in R1 and the antecedent of the zero form in R3. The topic could be virtually replaced by a single demonstrative pronoun "这/这个" without any change in the meaning of the CIPT clause.

As can be seen from the above examples，qualitative analysis is involved in this phase. For each chunk token，eight contextual clauses are examined for semantic relations. When semantic relations in all chunks are identified and when relevant values and symbols are recorded，it is necessary to represent the values and symbols in a way that they can be conveniently processed by the computer. Since my intent is to explore distribution of discoursal associations on the part of CIP topics in the corpus data and to obtain an empirical description of them，diagrams like those given in Figure 6.2 and 6.3，useful as they are when semantic connections are explained，are of little help in this respect. A form of matrix suitable for statistical analysis is thus adopted. It gives a clearer representation of the coding of semantic relations. Table 6.1 below is a sample of such a matrix created on the basis of the instances discussed above.

Table 6.1　Sample of data with coded semantic relations

No.	Category	Type	L4	L3	L2	L1	Token	R1	R2	R3	R4	Position
1.	NPbare	B	x	3	x	1	服装要改革/	1	2	3	4	090830
2.	NPmod	A	x	x	x	x	其实那一二一游行很多学生都去参加了/	1	2	3	4	040720
3.	NPdet	B	x	3	2	1	这块砖多出来了以后呢/	x	x	3	4	113050
4.	DEM	C	x	3	2	1	那个是在开始时候没有想到的/	x	x	x	x	022946
5.	NPdet	C	x	x	2	1	这个话实际上是生活当中曹家人当时说过的话/	1	x	3	x	233330

The matrix fulfils two functions. First, when viewed horizontally, the values and symbols show what positions the connected and unconnected contextual clauses are occupying within a discourse chunk. Second, a statistical investigation of the values and symbols in a vertical way can be automatically carried out and frequencies of the connected and unconnected contextual clauses be calculated. Such functions are indispensable for the study of discoursal associations of CIP topics. Moreover, the variable for CIP topic categories identified in chapter 4 and that for CIPT clause types identified in chapter 5 are retained in the matrix so that the data can be processed for different purposes and that more detailed descriptions of discoursal associations will be achieved. This means that discoursal associations can be examined in relation to either CIP topic category or to CIPT clause type. In this way, the research being conducted in this part is related to that already carried out in the previous two chapters and forms an extension of that at the discourse level. For practical purposes, CIPT clauses of type C are not further distinguished in this part. Tokens of subtypes CA and CB are all labeled as type C. Thus, discoursal associations, when examined in relation to CIPT clause types, will be investigated and described based on classification of CIPT clauses into type A, type B and type C. For each type, a separate sub-corpus is established. Accordingly, three sub-corpora A, B and C are created.

6.4   Semantic connection revisited

This section is intended to give a detailed explanation of how semantic connections are identified and analyzed drawing mainly on Halliday and Hasan's (1976) cohesion theory—specifically their ideas about lexical cohesion. Analyses are also made drawing on Hoey's (1983; 1991) theories of discourse analysis and of lexical repetition. Liu (2002) is referred to when distinguishing expressions are examined. In addition, semantic connection realized by general nouns in bare form is recognized here based on Liao's (1986) view on co-reference in text.

The data used for this part are discourse chunks collected from natural speech. Yet, they still possess the most important discourse property, coherence, though local in this case rather than global. This presupposes that within a chunk, semantic connections can be identified between the topic or an element in the topic and constituents in the contextual clauses. In the attempt to investigate how CIP topics fulfill discourse functions, I choose to focus on connections of this kind while neglecting connections among constituents in the contextual clauses.

Semantic connections are primarily conceptual. Their realizations rely heavily on linguistic means—lexis. This is why topics or elements contained in topics and contextual constituents are morphologically examined. The process of seeking semantic or conceptual connections is in essence the process of seeking linguistic means related in sense. The two processes occur simultaneously and are intertwined before discoursal associations of CIP topics are eventually investigated and described.

6. 4. 1　Lexical reiteration

Halliday and Hasan (1976:278) claim that "reiteration is a form of lexical cohesion which involves the repetition of a lexical item, at one end of the scale; the use of a general word to refer back to a lexical item, at the other end of the scale; and a number of things in between—the use of a synonym, near-synonym, or superordinate". The cohesive relations that fall under lexical reiteration have one commonality: the related items have the same referent. Consider the following examples, discussed by Halliday and Hasan (ibid):

(6) There was a large *mushroom* growing near her, about the same height as herself; and when she had looked under it, it occurred to her that she might as well look and see what was on the top of it.
She stretched herself up on tiptoe, and peeped over the edge of the *mushroom*, . . .

(7) Accordingly. . . I took leave, and turned to the *ascent* of the peak. The *climb* is perfectly easy. . .

(8) Then quickly rose Sir Bedivere, and ran,
And leaping down the ridges lightly, plung'd
Among the bulrush beds, and clutch'd the *sword*
And lightly wheel'd and threw it. The great *brand*
Made light'nings in the splendour of the moon. . .

(9) Henry's bought himself a new *Jaguar*. He practically lives in the *car*.

Repetition occurs in (6) where the second *mushroom* refers back to the first *mushroom*. Synonymous relation exists between *ascent* and *climb* in (7). In (8), *brand* is a near synonym of *sword*. Lastly in (9), *car* is a superordinate of *Jaguar*. In each of the four instances, the two related nouns have the same referent. Instances of such types are found in my own corpus data:

(10) L1 这是*我一直困惑的问题*/问题要让陈院长来解答/

(11) L1……叫做潢海铁网山上出产的一种*檀木*/这个木料原来是谁订的货呀/

(12) 两本书是同时写的/R1 所以读者会发现说写《*孩子你慢慢来*》的那个作者是温柔得不得了的一个女子/R2 但是写《*野火*》的是你刚刚说的就是非常张牙舞爪的很厉害的人/

In example (10), the bare noun in TOP "问题" is a simple repetition of the head of the objective noun phrase in the preceding contextual clause L1. Though in bare noun form, it has the same referent as the noun phrase "我一直困惑的问题" does. In (11), the head noun "木料" of the topic is a superordinate term of "檀木" in clause L1. The determiner "这个" helps to narrow down the scope of what "木料" refers to so that the topicalized noun phrase as a whole has the same referent as "檀木" does. Concerning example (12), analysis is made based on Hoey's (1983) view of Preview-Detail relation—part of his theory on discourse study—since it better explains the relation holding between the topicalized item "两本书" and the two succeeding book titles "*孩子你慢慢来*" and "*野火*". Hoey (1983:138-143) contends that the Preview-Detail relation is a type of General-Particular relation. Of the two elements of this relation, the Preview element may contain no clue that it constitutes part of a relation with a subsequent Detail element. Sometimes the Preview element may contain a clue in the form of listing, the extreme form of which is enumeration. A typical example of such case is seen in the following citation from Hoey (1983:139):

(13) I think then that the language of verse may be divided into three kinds. The first and highest is poetry proper, the language of inspiration... The second kind I call Parnassian. It can only be spoken by poets, but is not in the highest sense poetry... The third kind is merely the language of verse as distinct from that of prose, Delphic, the tongue of the Sacred Plain, I may call it...

The Preview element "three kinds" in the beginning clause of the chunk serves to signal that particular points are to be enumerated in the space to follow. Its relatedness to the subsequent discourse is embodied by the occurrence of the serial items "The first", "The second kind" and "The third kind" that provide specific information about what is previewed. Normally, the Preview is a noun phrase. In the same vein here, the noun phrase in TOP "两本书" in (12) is the Preview and the two book titles "孩子你慢慢来" and "野火" are the Details. The topic is semantically related to the two titles through Preview-Detail relation and establishes rightward associations with clauses R1 and R2.

As for cases where items involved do not have the same referent, Halliday and Hasan (1976:284) further argue that "it is not by virtue of any referential relation that there is a cohesive force set up between two occurrences of a lexical item; rather, the cohesion exists as a direct relation between the forms themselves (and thus is more like substitution than reference)". This is borne out by the example below (ibid):

(14) Henry presented her with his own portrait. As it happened, she had always wanted a portrait of Henry.

The first *portrait* has a definite reference while the second has an indefinite reference. Yet the second is still cohesive with the first. Similar instances are found in my own corpus data as well. Consider the following repeated from section 6.3.3:

(15) ……所以服装要改革/R1 不但要学匈奴人骑射的服装/R2 而且服装本身要紧身/

"服装" in the three clauses in (15) does not have the same referent. Yet, based on Halliday and Hasan, they are cohesively related. Although cohesion theory applies here, Hoey's view has more explanatory power at this point since it delves into the phenomenon more elaborately. Hoey (1991) divides lexical repetition into several types: simple lexical repetition, complex lexical repetition, simple paraphrase and complex paraphrase. Lexical repetition is also realized by superordinate, hyponymic, and co-reference expressions. Other ways of repeating include the use of personal pronouns, demonstrative pronouns and some words like *one*, *do* and *so that function as substitutes. Simple lexical repetition can be established when items involved are graphologically or phonologically identical and when they have the same referent. Common reference, however, is not an obligatory property of lexical repetition. If items involved do not have the same referent, the relationship* of simple repetition between them still stands when two questions can be answered affirmatively (Hoey 1991:59): i) Are the meanings of the items the same? In other words, is a paraphrase of one item a paraphrase of the other? ii) Do the items share a common context, or are their contexts related in some way? Accordingly, the two questions are prerequisites to be satisfied when simple repetition is assumed to be present between non-coreferential items. As far as (15) is concerned, the two pairs of "服装" can be marked as lexical repetition since they well meet the two pre-conditions.

Semantic connections are also identified when items involved fall within different syntactic categories rather than within the same category. Take the example below:

(16) A:L2 三年的工夫就*捅破了*一层窗户纸/
　　　B:L1 哎*捅破了*一层窗户纸/
　　　A:但是<u>这纸什么时候捅破的</u>也不知道/
　　　B:R1 哎怎么*捅破Ø*的不知道/

In this discourse chunk, the constituent in TOP is the embedded clause "这纸什么时候捅破的". The predicate verb "捅破" in the topic is, on the one hand, a simple repetition of the verbs occurring in the two preceding contextual clauses and, on the other hand, is repeated in the subsequent contextual clause. This chain of connection co-exists with another chain that embraces such nominal elements and a zero form as "这纸——一层窗户纸——Ø". The discourse associations of the topic are thus established.

6.4.2　Lexical collocation

Scholars are divided in interpreting collocation. For Firth (1957/1988:97), collocations of a given word are statements of the habitual or customary places of that word in collocational order but not in any other contextual order and emphatically not in any grammatical order. The collocation of a word or 'piece' is not to be regarded as mere juxtaposition, it is an order of mutual expectancy. Bolinger and Sears (1981:53) note that "a child asked to say the first thing that comes to mind on hearing the word *throw* will say *ball* rather than *toss*, and if asked to define a *hole* will say a *hole in the ground*". Such associations are characteristic of collocations and are linearly expressed in syntax. Robins (1989: 64-65) argues that collocation is the habitual association of a word in a language with other particular words in sentences. For this scholar, though collocations like *dark night* and *bright day* are undoubtedly related to the referential and situational meaning of the words concerned, collocation and situational meaning form different parts of what is stated by the use of words. Sometimes collocations are habitual but not associated with extralinguistic reference. *White* in *white fib* and *blue* in *blue streak* are such cases that have no reference to the actual colors. Reasonable as the above insights are, they are confined to collocations on sentence or clause level or phrase level. By contrast, Halliday and Hasan's view on collocation is more systematic and applicable for analyzing semantic relatedness between items on discourse level.

Collocating items that regularly co-occur in a discourse definitely contribute to the textual quality of the discourse. In Halliday and Hasan (1976:285), semantically related items that form collocational cohesion may cluster in diverse ways as: complementaries such as *boy...girl*, *stand up...sit down*, antonyms such as *like...hate*, *wet...dry*, *crowded...deserted*, converses such as *order...obey*, and co-hyponyms such as *chair...table*. Other collocational items include: pairs of words drawn from the same ordered series such as *Tuesday... Thursday* and *dollar...cent*; words drawn from unordered lexical sets like *basement...roof*, *road...rail*. Collocating words may be related as part to whole like *car...brake* or as part to part like *mouth...chin*. Items of word pairs such as *laugh...joke*, *blade...sharp*, *garden...dig* are in proximity in occurrence though their semantic relations are difficult to classify.

The discourse chunks used in this study provide a rich reserve where discoursal associations on the part of CIP topics are established through the use of collocations of various types. Consider the following:

(17) ……秦可卿的丧事都办完了/R1 皇帝都派了大太监亲予上祭了/

（18）L3 就像我们这个*摄影*镜头一样/L2 我把那个大山大水的背景*照*下来了/L1 然后把一些社会生活内容也*照*下来了/然后<u>两个底版一重叠</u>/R1 就洗出来了/

（19）L1 我就爱唱*滑稽*/他说*文明戏*你唱了以后/R1 大世界里面全是*滑稽*……

（20）<u>扑克牌我不会</u>/R1 *麻将牌*我不会/

（21）A：<u>房子给了小儿子</u>/

B：R1 原来父亲早就把自己名下的*所有财产*全部都给了这个小弟弟/

In example（17），"丧事"，as the head of the noun phrase in TOP and the predicate expression "上祭" in contextual clause R1 belong to different syntactic categories. Nonetheless，a close semantic relation holds between the two items. "丧事" means a series of funeral arrangements when someone passes away. The verb phrase "上祭" means to hold a memorial ceremony for the deceased who，when alive，enjoys a high social status or is from a noble family. It depicts activities involved in the funeral arrangements. The common context that the two items share licenses their semantic relatedness as collocation. Hence the topic，as a whole，achieves rightward association with clause R1. In（18），such expressions as "摄影镜头" in L3，"照" repeatedly in L2 and L1，"两个底版" in the CIPT clause and"洗" in R1 belong to the same lexical set. "两个底版" is in collocation with all the other items and acquires discoursal associations in both directions. Items "滑稽" and "文明戏" in（19）are co-hyponyms of the superordinate term "drama". The topicalized noun phrase "文明戏" thus bears discoursal association in both ways. The same is true of the relation holding between "扑克牌" and "麻将牌" in example（20）. The two items can be considered co-hyponyms of the superordinate term "game". The topic "扑克牌" stands in rightward association with R1. In fact，R1 is a felicitous CIPT clause，too，and is so recorded in the corpus. Viewing from the angle of the clause "麻将牌我不会" when it is treated as a CIPT clause，"麻将牌" becomes the topic and "扑 克 牌 我 不 会" becomes contextual clause L1. In this case，with the semantic relation holding between "扑克牌" and "麻将牌" unchanged，"麻将牌" conversely has leftward association with L1. In（21），there stands a part-whole relation between the topicalized bare noun "房子" in the underlined CIPT clause and the noun phrase "所有财产" in R1. Such collocational connection provides the noun "房子" with rightward discoursal association with clause R1.

6.4.3 Distinguishing expressions

Expressions like "别的", "其他" and "其余" in Chinese are equivalent to the indefinite pronoun "other" or "others" in English. Liu (2002: 170) terms such expressions as distinguishing pronouns. They deserve the term in that they are a special type of items used to distinguish people, objects or things from those already specified in the preceding discourse. When standing alone without modifying another item, "其他" and "其余" are for the most part followed by the nominalizing particle "*de*" and, like "别的", form "*de*" structures (equivalent to noun phrases) referring to the remaining ones or part of a whole distinct from or in contrast with what has been previously mentioned. When used as a modifier, the accompanied head is often a general noun and the entire noun phrase has the same reference as the corresponding "*de*" construction does.

Before taking a closer look at semantic connections realized by distinguishing expressions, it is neccesary to review some well-known analyses of "other" in English in the literature. Halliday and Hasan (1976: 78-79) treat "other" as expressing general comparative reference both cataphorically and anaphorically as in the following instances:

(22) The <u>other</u> squirrels hunted up and down the nut bushes; but <u>Nutkin</u> gathered robin's pincushions off a briar bush, and stuck them full of pine-needle pins.

(23) They've given us <u>special places in the front row</u>. Would you prefer the other seats?

While making a comparison, "other" is cataphorically cohesive with "Nutkin" in (22) and anaphorically cohesive with "special places in the front row" in (23). In Quirk et al. (1985), the comparative use of "other" is interpreted in a different way. Consider:

(24) I don't have any other cups than those ((that/which) I have) in the sink.

Example (24) is cited from Quirk et al. (1985: 1136). "Other" as a determiner here conveys a comparison between two classes of cups—cups in the sink and cups not in the sink—within the clause boundaries. Thus, it is hard to assume that "other" exerts any cohesive effect. In Hoey (1991:74), "other", "another" and "the other" are interpreted from the angle of discourse study. They are treated as demonstrative modifiers and analyzed in three ways. First, if they accompany a lexical item in a repetition link with an earlier item, their linking function is ignored to avoid double accounting. Second, if the item they accompany is in no such relation, they are treated as creating a link. Third, when "the other" and "another" occur without an accompanying lexical item as head, they are considered as marking the presence of ellipsis. As far as discoursal associations on the part of CIP topics are concerned in the present study, Hoey's view is of much help and thus forms the basis of the rules followed in the process of data analysis in this section. The rules are: i) within a CIP topic, when "别的", "其他" or "其余" accompanies a lexical item that stands in a semantic relation with an earlier or subsequent item, the constituent in TOP as a whole is considered as establishing connection to that item; ii) when "别的", "其他" or "其余" occurs alone, or "其他" and "其余" occur in the form of "*de*" construction, without accompanying a lexical item as head, they are all considered as serving to connect an earlier or subsequent item. At this point, these pronouns' function of embodying semantic relations is emphasized while their grammatical function of marking the presence of ellipsis is of minor importance. Consider the following instances from my own corpus data:

(25) L4 他就把*画* 截下来/L3 单独裱 Ø 在一块木板上/L2 就把它贴在木板上/ L1 展出*那个* /其他东西他们就一般就不展出了/

(26) L2 他是个*教授* /L1 规规矩矩*教书* /别的事情都不管/

(27) 别的不会想/R1 这个最熟悉/

(28) ……L1 一般就是帮着他*收拾收拾碗筷什么的* /其余的他就不让我做了/

In (25), the CIP topic "其他东西" consists of the modifier "其他" and the general noun "东西". The referent of the entire noun phrase is in contrast with the referent of the demonstrative "那个" in L1. The topic is hence treated as standing in semantic relation with "那个". Since "那个", the pronoun "它" in L2 and the zero form Ø in L3 all refer anaphorically to "画" in L4, the topic is, by

126

transitivity, treated as standing in semantic relations with "它" in L2, Ø in L3 and "画" in L4 as well. When the connections are coded, values "1", "2", "3" and "4" are respectively assigned. In (26), the noun phrase in TOP "别的事情" refers to things distinct from "教书". The two elements form a contrast. The topic is thus semantically related to "教书". Since "教书" and "教授" are in collocation, by transitivity, "别的事情" is considered being semantically related to "教书", too. Different from the above, in (27), the topic "别的" is cataphorically related to "这个" in R1 and the referents of the two items are mutually exclusive. In (28), the topicalized "*de*" construction "其余的" forms a contrast with "收拾收拾碗筷什么的". The two constituents are therefore semantically related. In reality, no instance is found in the corpus in which an item modified by "别的", "其他" or "其余" does not bear a semantic relation with an earlier or subsequent item. It is evident that when a distinguishing item is embraced in a topic, there is an overwhelming tendency for the topic to acquire discoursal associations, either leftward or rightward.

6.4.4　Mixed connections

Within a discourse chunk, semantic connections may sometimes be realized in a mixed way. Namely, a topic or an item contained in a topic may be semantically related to a constituent in a contextual clause through lexical reiteration and meanwhile related to a constituent in another contextual clause through lexical collocation. The occurrence of mixed connections does not affect value assignment. Consider：

(29) ……L2 就是苏联*出版*工作的经验/L1*那个*专家不会翻/俄语专家他怎么知道版口这个词怎么说/R1 这个校对中间*这些行话*他不会说/R2 那么搞*出版*专业的人又不懂俄语/

Example (29) contains three CIPT clauses. Only the underlined one is discussed for the time being while the other two, i.e., clauses L1 and R1 are ignored. The CIPT clause in question is an embedded one and the topic "版口这个词" is an apposition construction. Towards the left of the topic structure, the appositive "版口" collocates with the item "出版" in L2 and stands in a semantic relation with it. The demonstrative "那个" in L1 anaphorically refers to the noun phrase "苏联出版

工作的经验" in L2 in which "出版" occurs. The appositive "版口" is thus treated as, by transitivity, being related to "那个". Clauses L1 and L2 are respectively assigned value "1" and "2". Towards the right of the topic structure, "这些行话" in clause R1 is a general noun phrase that covers "版口这个词" as a specific term. Or when viewed as a definite noun phrase, "这些行话" is a simple paraphrase of "版口这个词". The item "出版" recurs in clause R2 and collocates with the appositive"版口". The topic hence acquires associations with both clauses R1 and R2. Consider another case in which mixed connections appear:

(30) <u>至于背后的犯罪呢它无权更好地查处</u>/R1 它只能*查*完了 Ø 以后/R2 再 Ø 移交检察院立案/R3 由检察院重新*侦查*Ø/

In (30), three zero forms occur respectively in R1, R2 and R3. Yet, their referents are different. In R1, the zero form "Ø" refers back to the head of the topic "犯罪". The zero form in R2, preceded by the covert element "把", has the same referent. The zero form in R3, however, anaphorically refers to the entire topic "背后的犯罪". Conversely, we can say that the topic is repeated in different ways in the subsequent discourse. Meanwhile, "犯罪" collocates with such elements as "查处" in R1, "立案" in R2 and "侦查" in R3, all of which bestow on the topic rightward associations.

6.4.5 Di-and split-connections

When two items of a contextual clause that belong to different syntactic categories are simultaneously related to the topic in a chunk, the coding of the association between that contextual clause and the topic, as shown in the above analysis of (30), remains the same. The value assigned to the clause is not affected. Conversely, value assignment is not affected either when syntagmatic items of a topic stand in separate semantic relations with different elements of a given contextual clause. This is what is meant by di-connection. Consider:

(31) A:L2 三年的工夫就*捅破*了一层窗户纸/
　　B:L1 哎*捅破*了一层窗户纸/
　　A:但是这纸什么时候捅破的也不知道/
　　B:R1 哎怎么*捅破*Ø 的不知道/

Example (31) is repeated from (16). The CIP topic "这纸什么时候捅破的" is an embedded clause. The items "这纸" and "捅破" are used figuratively. Still，their semantic relations can be identified. The definite noun phrase "这纸" refers anaphorically to "一层窗户纸" that occurs in both L1 and L2. It then becomes the antecedent of the zero form in R1. "捅破" in the topic is a simple lexical repetition of the predicate verb in both L1 and L2 and is further repeated in R1. The semantic relations are represented diagrammatically in Figure 6.4 below：

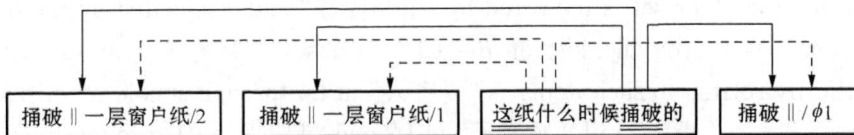

| 捅破‖一层窗户纸/2 | 捅破‖一层窗户纸/1 | 这纸什么时候捅破的 | 捅破‖/φ1 |

Figure 6.4　Recording of di-connection and value assignment

The two sets of arrow lines (one set consisting of normal arrow lines and the other set of dot arrow lines) represent two sets of semantic relations. One set is triggered by "这纸" and designated by the dot lines. The other set is triggered by "捅破" and designated by the normal lines. The fact that each contextual clause in the excerpt is pointed at by two lines，i.e.，twice associated with the topic，does not affect the value assigned to that clause.

Split-connection means that items of a topic，belonging to different syntactic categories，form separate semantic relations with elements that occur in different contextual clauses. Consider：

(32) ……L4 目的是想安抚受害人 /L3 洗去嫌疑 /L2 现在王培君的案子已经了结了 /L1 于是荣自立就要起诉她还房子 /受害人在上当受骗后做出这样的猜测是完全可以理解的 /R1 而且戎自立的举动确实也很让人疑惑 /R2 那么戎自立到底参没参与诈骗 /R3 事发后为什么主动地提出还钱、让房呢 /

Example (32) is extracted from a discourse chunk. The topic is also an embedded clause. The expressions "受害人" and "上当受骗" in the topic are of different syntactic categories. Different from "这纸" and "捅破" in (30)，they stand in separate semantic relations with items in different contextual clauses. Such connections are shown in the diagram below：

129

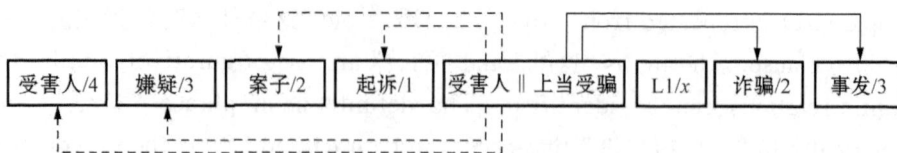

Figure 6.5　Recording of split-connection and value assignment

Here again two sets of semantic relations are identified (indicated by two sets of arrow lines). One set is triggered by "受害人" and designated by the dot arrow lines while the other set is triggered by "上当受骗" and designated by the normal arrow lines. Towards the left of the CIPT clause, "受害人" in the topic is semantically related to such items as "受害人" in L4 through simple repetition (受害人—受害人), "嫌疑" in L3, "案子" in L2 and "起诉" in L1 through collocation (嫌疑—受害人，案子—受害人，起诉—受害人). As far as the rightward discourse is concerned, the item "诈骗" in R2 is semantically related to "上当受骗" in the topic through complex lexical repetition (上当受骗—诈骗) and the general noun "事" in R3 related to it through anaphoric reference (事—上当受骗).① Arrow lines of different sets do not converge on any one of the clauses in the chunk. This

---

① The interpretation of general nouns fulfilling cohesive function in discourse is two-folded (cf., Halliday and Hasan 1976: 274-276). On the one hand, a general noun is a lexical means when used as a superordinate item. Hoey (1991: 69) acknowledges such an organizing feature on the condition that a superordinate item occurs ahead of its hyponym but not vice virsa. On the other hand, a general noun is a grammatical means when used to, being preceded by the definite article "the", co-refer with a previously evoked element. Though a clear distinguishing line between the two aspects is not easy to draw, Liao (1986: 45-61) gives an in-depth examination of general nouns in Chinese focusing more on the grammatical aspect. He points out that the element that a general noun, taking a demonstrative as modifier, is coreferential with, can be a noun, a verb, a clause or even a paragraph. The following instances are cited from Liao (ibid):

In instance i, the underlined noun phrases "这种人" and "第三者" have the same referent. In ii, the noun phrase "这一目标" anaphorically refers to the act expressed by the verb phrase "解放生产力". The noun phrase "这个问题" in iii refers to the sequence of clauses that occur in the preceding discourse. Occasionally, a general noun in the bare form, like "事", can be used in the same way as shown in the instance below (ibid):

i. 第三者的行为是不道德的，这种人把自己的幸福建筑在他人的不幸和痛苦之上，为了满足自己的私欲，不惜破坏他人的婚姻幸福。

ii. 邓小平同志强调指出：改革科技体制是为了解放生产力。从这一目标出发，就要逐步使技术开发研究面向经济。

iii. 我国森林面积小，覆盖率低，水土流失严重，生态平衡的状况越来越差。这个问题，如果再不加以有效地解决，就将犯下影响子孙后代的历史性错误。

iv. 此(1985年1月11日)前不久，一枚从巴伦支海发射的苏联 SS-N-3 型巡航导弹闯进挪威北部领空，飞越挪威、芬兰边界后，坠落在芬兰北部。事发后，挪威、芬兰提出抗议，苏联后来表示道歉。

is borne out diagrammatically by the fact that the dotted arrow lines and the normal arrow lines in Figure 6.5 point to opposite directions. This is where di-connection and split-connection differ. Still, value assignment follows the same rules.

6.4.6 Poset relation

Up to this point, various types of semantic relations occurring in the corpus data have been analyzed drawing on theories about lexical connection. One other theory that is deliberately ignored in this study is poset (partially ordered set) theory (Birner and Ward 1998; Gregory and Michaelis 2001) though it specifically concerns semantic relations holding between information presented in different clauses. 'Poset' is a concept borrowed from the mathematical discipline known as set theory. Roughly, a partial order is an order on a set A, i.e., a binary relation (expressed as "$\leqslant$") on A with the following properties (Geng and Qu 1990:169-172):

(33) i. Reflexive: for all $x \in A$, $x \leqslant x$
    ii. Antisymmetric: $(x \leqslant y) \wedge (y \leqslant x) => x = y$
    iii. Transitive: $(x \leqslant y) \wedge (y \leqslant z) => x \leqslant z$

Set A together with the partial order on it is called poset.

When employed in the explanation of relations that hold between a preposed element A and an evoked entity B, a poset relation means that A and B can be related in one of three possible ways: "A can represent a lower value than does B, A can represent a higher value than does B, or A and B can be of equal rank, or 'alternate values' sharing a common higher or lower value but not ordered with respect to each other" (Birner and Ward 1998:18). The relations are exemplified in the following instances:

(34) a. Lower value
        G: Do you like this album?
        M: Yeah, this song I really like.
    b. Higher value
        C: Have you filled out the Summary Sheet?
        T: Yeah. Both the Summary Sheet and the Recording Sheet I've done.
    c. Alternate values

G: Did you get any more [answers to the crossword puzzle]?

S: No. The cryptogram I can do like that. The crossword puzzle is hard.

(Birner and Ward 1998:18-19)

In (34a), the preposed noun phrase *this* song marks the poset relation of "is-a-part-of" to the noun phrase *this album* in the preceding clause. The referent of the former represents a lower value than that of the latter within the poset {album part}. In (34b), the constituent *the Summary Sheet and the Recording Sheet* stands in a poset relation to *the Summary Sheet* and represents a higher value than the latter within the poset {forms}. Birner and Ward term *the Summary Sheet and the Recording Sheet* a superset, which contains *the Summary Sheet* as a member. The relation between the two elements also licenses the description of "whole-part". In (34c), within the poset {newspaper puzzles}, *the crossword puzzle* and *the cryptogram* are alternate, equally-ranked values, presenting a relation of "is-a-type-of". Their relation can also be described as "co-hyponyms" of a superordinate term "newspaper puzzles". Other types of relations, like entity/attribute, type/subtype, set/subset, and equality, are included in poset relations by Birner and Ward (1998:19). It is evident that this theory covers fewer phenomena than cohesion theory does. Further, it is primarily applicable to the analysis of semantic connection between a preposed element and a previously evoked one, i.e., leftward connection, rather than connections in both ways. Accordingly, poset relation is not referred to in the present study.

6.4.7   Data analysis

When all the 217 tokens are examined—all semantic relations are identified and checked through which CIP topics acquires discoursal associations—and corresponding values or symbols assigned, data analyses are carried out in each sub-corpus using Microsoft Excel tool. The research in this phase is a quantitative one. It is conducted on the matrices constructed categorically aiming to obtain a series of statistics that will help depict the associations from different angles.

6.5   Discoursal associations on the part of CIP topics

In this section, results of the investigations into discoursal associations on the part of CIP topics are presented. They concern five aspects: i) distribution of associated contextual clauses on both left and right sides of CIPT clauses relative to syntactic type of CIPT clauses and a comparison; ii) distribution of associated contextual clauses relative to position in discourse chunks in each sub-corpus; iii) a comparison between NP topics and pooled topics with respect to their discoursal associations; iv) a comparison among NPdet topics (noun phrase topics that contain a demonstrative as determiner), NPmod topics (noun phrase topics that contain one modifier) and NPbare topics (bare noun topics) with respect to their discoursal associations; v) distribution of association patterns in the corpus data. These aspects will combine to answer the second sub-question of research question 2) posed in section 6.2 as well as to provide detailed and specific information on discourse properties of CIP topics.

6.5.1　Contextual clauses associated with CIP topics

Sorted data in each sub-corpus are investigated. Statistics reveals that contextual clauses associated with CIP topics stand more densely on the left side of CIPT clauses than on the right side. This is true in each of the three sub-corpora and with the pooled data as shown in Table 6.2 below.

Table 6.2　Distribution of contextual clauses associated with CIP topics

Sub-corpus	Total of contextual clauses (L)	Number of associated clauses (L)	% (L)	Total of contextual clauses (R)	Number of associated clauses (R)	% (R)
A (77)	308	172	55.8	308	157	51.0
B (79)	316	180	57.0	316	153	48.4
C (61)	244	152	62.3	244	117	48.0
Pooled (217)	868	504	58.1	868	427	49.2

The total of contextual clauses on the left and on the right side of CIPT clauses in a sub-corpus is obtained through multiplying x by 4. "x" is the number of tokens in the sub-corpus. "4" is the number of contextual clauses standing to the left and right of a CIPT clause. As can be seen in Table 6.2, 172 out of 308 leftward contextual clauses in sub-corpus A are discoursally associated with the topics. They account for 55. 8% of the total. By contrast, 157 out of 308 rightward contextual clauses in this sub-corpus are associated with the topics. These clauses account for 51. 0% of the same total. As for sub-corpus B, 180 leftward contextual clauses are found discoursally associated with the topics, accounting for 57.0% of a total of 316 while 153 rightward contextual clauses are associated, forming 48. 4% of the same total. In sub-corpus C, 152 leftward contextual clauses are identified as being discoursally associated, forming 62. 3% of a total of 244 while 117 rightward ones are identified as being so, accounting for 48.0%. When the data are put together, 504 leftward contextual clauses are found being associated with the topics while 427 rightward ones are so. The former and the latter respectively account for 58. 1% of the total 868 clauses on the left and 49. 2% on right. The distribution of leftward and rightward associations in the three sub-corpora is visually demonstrated in Figure 6. 6.

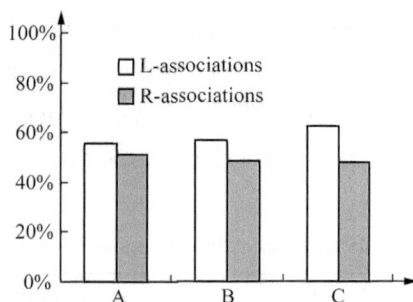

Figure 6. 6   Distribution of l-and r-associations and a comparison

In the graph above, each pair of bars for a specified sub-corpus represents the percentages of the two groups of contextually associated clauses in that sub-corpus: those to the left of CIPT clauses and those to the right. Evidently, all the left bars are taller than the right ones. This means that leftward associations outnumber rightward ones in all the three sub-corpora. When the gap is described in terms of mean number of clauses, the associations can be represented as follows:

The mean is calculated as:

Mean $= \sum x / N$.

"$\sum x$" is the total of the leftward or rightward clauses that are associated with the topics. "N" is the number of tokens in a sub-corpus. Table 6. 3 reveals that on average, 2.2 leftward clauses are associated with a topic in sub-corpus A while 2.0 rightward clauses are so. In sub-corpus B, 2.3 leftward clauses are associated while 1.9 rightward clauses are so. In sub-corpus C, the corresponding numbers are 2.5 and 1.9. Of the three pairs of figures listed, the difference between the last pair is the biggest. This implies that topics in type C clauses have stronger tendency to be semantically related to entities in the preceding than in the succeeding clauses.

Table 6.3   Mean number of contextual clauses associated with CIP topics

Sub-corpus	Number of tokens	Mean number of L-associated clauses	Mean number of R-associated clauses
A	77	2.2	2.0
B	79	2.3	1.9
C	61	2.5	1.9

A question then further arises: how do the associated clauses distribute on both sides of CIPT clauses in each of the three sub-corpora? In other words, how do the clauses distribute in different positions within the discourse chunks? The answer to the question in essence contributes more to the understanding of discoursal association patterns of CIP topics and will be discussed in a separate part.

6.5.2   Distribution of associated clauses in relation to position

When associated contextual clauses in different positions are counted by means of values assigned and percentages of corresponding values calculated, distribution of such clauses relative to position in each sub-corpus emerges as shown in Table 6.4 and 6.5.

Table 6.4   Distribution of leftward associations

Sub-corpus	L4		L3		L2		L1	
	N	%	N	%	N	%	N	%
A(308)	29	9.4	35	11.4	47	15.3	61	19.8
B(316)	31	9.8	40	12.7	48	15.2	61	19.3
C(244)	28	11.5	30	12.3	45	18.4	49	20.1

Table 6. 5   Distribution of rightward associations

Sub-corpus	R1		R2		R3		R4	
	N	%	N	%	N	%	N	%
A(308)	53	17.2	45	14.6	34	11.0	25	8.1
B(316)	51	16.1	43	13.6	33	10.4	26	8.2
C(244)	38	15.6	32	13.1	25	10.2	22	9.0

In the tables above, positions of associated contextual clauses are listed as variables in the first row in the form of "Letter + Number". The figure under "N" shows the specified amount of associated clauses that occur in the stated position in a sub-corpus. The figure under "%" shows the proportion of the specified amount of associated clauses in that position. Figures in Table 6. 4 spread increasingly from left to right, or to be exact, from L4 to L1. In contrast, figures in Table 6. 5 spread decreasingly from left to right, or from R1 to R4. Based on the above statistics, Figure 6. 7 provides graphic representations of distribution of associated contextual clauses in the three sub-corpora.

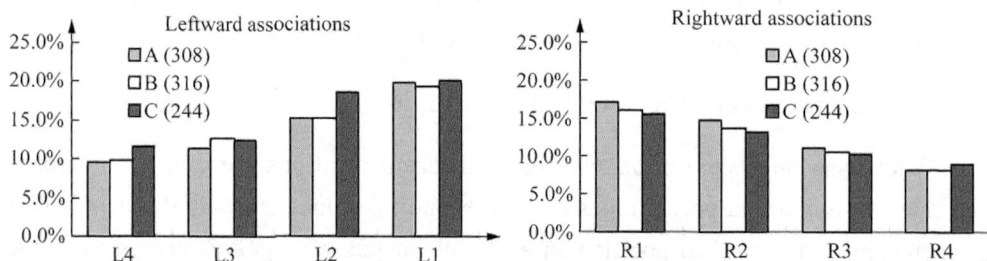

Figure 6. 7   Distribution of l- and r-associations relative to position

The graphs in Figure 6. 7 visually depict distribution of both leftward and rightward contextual clauses associated with the topics. They are deliberately put side by side to give a comparative demonstration of the association patterns. Between the two graphs stand the imaginary CIPT clauses. Both graphs show that in each of the three sub-corpora, the frequency of associated contextual clauses on either side varies when position varies. Namely, the closer a position is to the CIPT clause, the higher the frequency of associated clauses is in that position, or,

136

the greater the number of associations is in that position. Put in a different way, the nearer a contextual clause stands to the CIPT clause, the stronger the tendency is for the clause to be associated with the CIP topic. Moreover, frequencies of the associated contextual clauses on both sides of CIPT clauses do not distribute symmetrically in the sub-corpora though positions of the contextual clauses do stand symmetrically. A leftward frequency in a certain position is higher than the rightward frequency in its counterpart position. For example, when comparing the frequency of associated contextual clauses in position L1 and that in position R1 in sub-corpus A, the frequency in the former position is higher than that in the latter. This is true of paired frequencies in other paired positions in this sub-corpus as well as in the other two sub-corpora even when the difference between the members of a pair is minute, say, the difference between the frequency in L3 (11.4) and that in R3 (11.0) in sub-corpus A.

6.5.3 NP topics vs pooled topics: a comparison

It is pointed out in chapter IV that noun phrase topics are prototypical and form the bulk of the topics under discussion. This makes necessary the exploration of discoursal associations on the part of noun phrase topics and a comparison in this respect between such topics and pooled topics. Presumably, distribution of discoursal associations manifested by prototypical NP topics is most representative of CIP topics as a whole in terms of discourse property. The comparison can provide a frame of reference for assessing associations that CIP topics of all types establish such that the description of discourse features of CIP topics is, overall, well grounded and reliable. When data bearing the code of "NP" category are singled out from each sub-corpus, they are put together instead of being distinguished and subsumed under different subtypes. Based on the semantic connections identified, the associations of NP topics are investigated in the same way as the associations of topics in each sub-corpus: the occurrences of associated clauses in different positions are counted and their frequencies calculated. The same is done with pooled topics for the purpose of a comparison. The results are presented in Table 6.6 and Table 6.7 below and visualized in Figure 6.8.

Table 6.6　NP-Ts vs pooled-Ts: a comparison of associations (L)

	L4		L3		L2		L1	
	N	%	N	%	N	%	N	%
NP(632)	61	9.7	74	11.7	102	16.1	123	19.5
All(868)	88	10.1	105	12.1	140	16.1	171	19.7

Table 6.7　NP-Ts vs pooled-Ts: a comparison of associations (R)

	R1		R2		R3		R4	
	N	%	N	%	N	%	N	%
NP(632)	102	16.1	90	14.2	71	11.2	52	8.2
All(868)	142	16.4	120	13.8	92	10.6	73	8.4

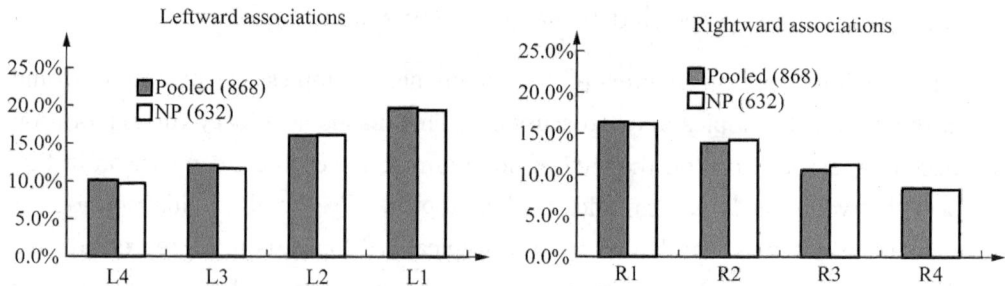

Figure 6.8　NP-Ts vs pooled-Ts: a comparison of associations (L and R)

The above tables summarize distribution of associated clauses in relation to position in discourse chunks for the two sets of data. It was expected that disparity might appear in one way or another. Surprisingly, no significant difference occurs. Compared to pooled topics, NP topics show a slightly weaker tendency to be semantically related to clauses in positions L4 and L3 while a slightly stronger tendency to be semantically related to clauses in positions R2 and R3. Difference in other positions is totally negligible. In the main, associations distribute in the two sets of data consistently. What is true earlier is also true here of the associations of NP topics: the nearer a position to the topic structure, the higher the frequency of the associations in that position. Likewise, leftward and rightward associations are not symmetrical: the former outnumber the latter. Considering that NP topics form the overwhelming majority of CIP topics, the association pattern on the part of NP topics therefore can be considered descriptive of CIP topics as a whole.

6.5.4　Prototypical subcategories of noun phrases in TOP

It is revealed earlier in Chapter 4 that three types of simple noun phrases— noun phrases that contain a demonstrative determiner (NPdet), noun phrases that contain one modifier (NPmod) and bare nouns (NPbare)—form prototypical subcategories of nominal phrases playing the role of CIP topics. Chen (1987) notes that NPdet units express definite reference and that NPmod units have a strong tendency to express definite reference depending on the specificity of the modifier. They are used anaphorically in discourse for the most part. However, a description of discourse properties of these units is definitely incomplete when their anaphoricity is vaguely interpreted while their cataphoricity not touched upon at all. As for NPbare topics, they exhibit anaphoricity as well as cataphoricity rather than express genericness, as discussed in section 6.3.3. This section is intended to be hole-mending in this regard through an empirical investigation of associations relative to position that the three kinds of units in TOP establish in discourse chunks. The results are depicted as follows.

Table 6.8　NPdet-, NPmod-and NPbare-Ts: a comparison of associations (L)

	L4		L3		L2		L1	
	N	%	N	%	N	%	N	%
NPdet(180)	20	11.1	22	12.2	27	15.0	38	21.1
NPmod(152)	16	10.5	16	10.5	26	17.1	31	20.4
NPbare(128)	11	8.6	17	13.3	17	13.3	25	19.5

Table 6.9　NPdet-, NPmod-and NPbare-Ts: a comparison of associations (R)

	R1		R2		R3		R4	
	N	%	N	%	N	%	N	%
NPdet(180)	26	14.4	19	10.6	19	10.6	13	7.2
NPmod(152)	28	18.4	24	15.8	22	14.5	14	9.2
NPbare(128)	18	14.1	18	14.1	13	10.2	10	7.8

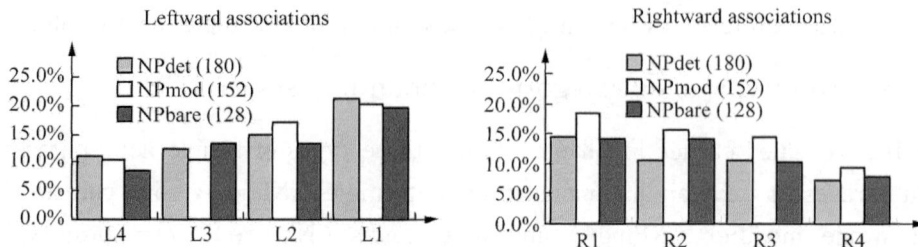

Figure 6. 9   NPdet-, NPmod-and NPbare-Ts: a comparison of associations (L and R)

Overall, distributions of associations in the three sets of data display the same tendency and are parallel with distributions revealed in the previous sections: associations figure more to the left of CIPT clauses than to the right. Nonetheless, noticeable divergence emerges in two ways. First, as shown in the tables, for each set of data, there is one pair of equal association frequencies appearing on the same side of topic structure. There are four such pairs in all, each pair being marked out by the same symbol. This weakens the observation on a small scale that the nearer a position to the topic structure, the more associations occur in that position. Yet, no incident is found in which associations in a position near to the topic structure are outnumbered by those in a more distant position when the positions are on the same side. Second, there are two incidents—one with NPmod topics, the other with NPbare topics—where associations in a leftward position are surpassed by those in its symmetric rightward position (L3-R3 for NPmod topics, L2-R2 for NPbare topics). This clashes to a degree with the pervasive phenomenon observed in this study that associations in a given leftward position outnumber those in its symmetric rightward position. Third, leftward associations on the part of NPdet topics do not tower considerably over those on the part of the other two types of topics. Admittedly, the anaphoricity of NPdet topics is much less strong than expected but has been overemphasized in the literature. By contrast, anaphoricity and cataphoriciry of NPbare topics are far stronger than expected considering that not much reference has been made to such traits to date. As for NPmod topics, rightward associations in all the four positions tower over those of the other types of topics. These topics hence exhibit a stronger tendency to be cataphoric.

6.5.5　Discoursal association patterns

Undoubtedly, there are three patterns for a CIP topic to be discoursally associated: leftward, rightward and in both directions. There is also the possibility that a CIP topic has no association in either direction. This part is devoted to the enquiry into the distribution of patterns in the corpus data. Investigation following this thought yields the results as shown in the table and graph below.

Table 6.10　Distribution of association patterns in the corpus

	Both leftward and rightward associations		Leftward associations only		Rightward associations only		No association	
	N	%	N	%	N	%	N	%
A(77)	64	29.5	7	3.2	6	2.8	0	0
B(79)	60	27.7	13	6.0	6	2.8	0	0
C(61)	47	21.7	12	5.5	1	0.5	1	0.5

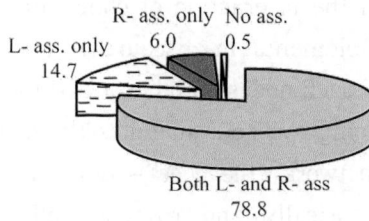

Figure 6.10　Distribution of association patterns in pooled data

According to Figure 6.10, topics that have discoursal associations in both directions are overwhelming in terms of frequency. Topics with no association in either direction are rare, occurring only once. In between them, topics that have leftward associations only occur occasionally, accounting for 14.7% of the total while topics with rightward associations only occur 13 times, making up 6.0% of the pooled data.

141

6.6 Discussion

6.6.1 Discoursal associations: a cognitive interpretation

The examinations above clearly manifest that as far as CIP topics are concerned, syntax and discourse are not separate and that CIPT clauses are functionally motivated. Discoursal associations are just a linguistic mechanism for the realization of coherence in discourse, "the degree to which different parts (words, sentences, paragraphs) of a text are connected to one another" (Carroll 2000:158). Associations as such in the external world are a demonstration of coherence in mind, the cognitive processes involved in producing discourse. From the perspective of cognition, coherence is a mental phenomenon. It is "a property of what emerges during speech production and comprehension—the mentally represented text, and in particular the mental processes that partake in constructing that mental representation (Gernsbacher and Givon 1995). The achievement of mental coherence relies heavily on the interaction of conceptual nodes that correspond to semantically interrelating elements in discourse. The nodes form members of different networks. One of such nodes matches a CIP topic or an item held in a CIP topic. The network embracing the node matches the dicourse chunk that contains the CIP topic. Within the network, the node is either anaphorically or cataphorically linked to, or both anaphorically and cataphorically linked to other nodes. Nonetheless, the linking points do not scatter randomly. Instead, they disperse in a way as being described by Collins and Loftus (1975) in their theory of spreading activation. The graph below (cited from Collins and Loftus 1975) is an illustration of the theory.

In the fragment of a semantic network depicted in Figure 6.11, interacting conceptual nodes like "sunrises" and "sunsets" stand closely to one another while non-interacting nodes like "flower" and "vehicle" stand distantly from one another. A shorter line represents greater relatedness. Supposing the node "sunrises" is activated, it will take less time for the activation to spread to the near nodes like "sunsets" or "clouds" than to the distant ones like "vehicle" or "street" In the mental network of a discourse chunk, the anaphoric linking of the topic node is presupposed by its inherent feature as given, activated or shared information. Namely,

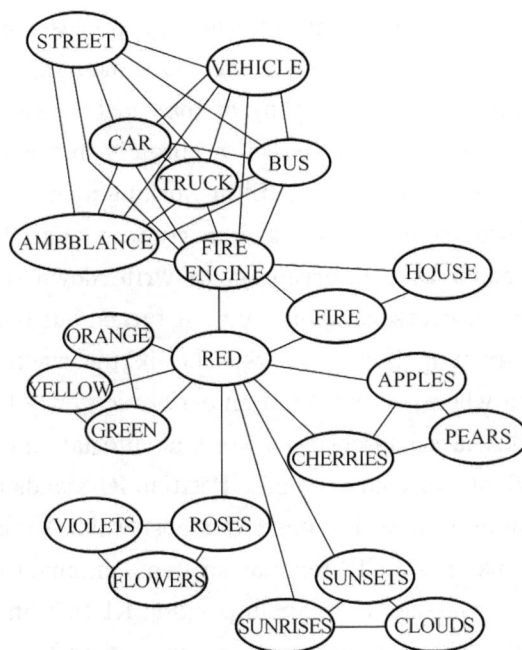

Figure 6. 11 A schematic representation of concept relatedness
in a stereotypical fragment of human memory

it is bound to be anaphoric due to its informational status as being given, activated
or shared. The anaphoric linkings of CIP topic nodes exhibit an accumulative
pattern of associations on the left of topic structures with their position moving
close to the structures. This is largely due to the fact that a topic node is more
easily linked to a near node than to a distant one when its activation spreads faster
to the former than to the latter. At this point, the principle of iconic proximity is
also of explanatory power. According to this principle, "elements which have a
close relationship must be placed together" (Ungerer and Schmid 2001:251-252).
While position L1 stands nearest to the CIPT clause on its left, an antecedent node
of the topic node shows the strongest tendency to occur in that position. Position
L4 stands farthest away from the CIPT clause. An antecedent or related node of
the topic node thus shows the weakest tendency to occur there. Positions L2 and
L3 stand between the nearest and farthest points. The linking tendencies for
antecedent or related nodes in those positions therefore will be hard to excel that in
position L1 but yet will always come before that in L4. Such a proximity-oriented

143

pattern undoubtedly has to do with information processing: the shorter the distance between a pair of linked nodes, the more mentally-accessible the latter node and the faster information processing of that node. Researchers believe that words presented at the end of a list recall accurately and exhibit recency effect because at the time of recall they were still in working memory (Howard 1983:93-101). Memory for discourse operates in a similarly way. A study reveals that when individuals were asked at each interruption to write down in verbatim form as much of the preceding discourse as they could, it turned out that the percentage of correct recall of the next to last clause was far better when it was part of the current sentence than when it was part of an earlier sentence (Carroll 2000:166).

The rightward discoursal associations are a manifestation of cataphoric linking in the mental network of a discourse chunk. Position R1 stands nearest to the CIPT clause on its right while position R4 stands farthest way. A node, if linked to the cataphoric node that matches a CIP topic or an item contained in a CIP topic, will show a much stronger tendency to occur in position R1 than in position R4. Again this can be attributed to the fact that it takes shorer time for a node in R1 than a node in R4 to spread its activation to the topic node. As for the other two positions, they are nearer to the CIPT clause than R4 but farther away from it than R1. The tendency for linked nodes to occur in those positions is hence weaker than the tendency for linked nodes to occur in R1 but stronger than that for linked nodes to occur in R4. In Givon (1983, 1993b, 1995b, 2001a), topic persistence is investigated as one of the two aspects of topicality—the other being referential distance—in order to reveal "how important the referent is going to be in the upcoming ('cataphoric') discourse" (1993b: 182). Topic persistence is also referred to as thematic importance. In the present study, the rightward association pattern is investigated to demonstrate how CIP topics behave cataphorically in the subsequent discourse so that the constituents, as a syntactic phenomenon, will be understood better in relation to their use in discourse and that their cognitive motivation is examined.

Compared to anaphoric linking, cataphoric linking is less intense. To a large extent, anaphoric linking is the impetus for the initialization or incomplete initialization of a CIP topic node such that the node is proximate to an antecedent or related node in the preceding mentally-represented discourse and that information processing is easier and smoother. Conversely, the clause-initial or near clause-initial position such a node occupies further enhances the node's chance of being anaphoric. This makes it a corollary that the leftward and rightward links are not symmetric and that the rightward links distribute more densely than the rightward links. The discoursal demonstration of this cognitive asymmetry is that the leftward associations outnumber the rightward ones.

6.6.2 Some thoughts on Gregory and Michaelis's study

In Gregory and Michaelis' (2001) comparative study on functional opposition between topicalization and left dislocation, the discoursal function of topicalization is depicted as: the majority of the preclausal-NP denotata in TOP are previously mentioned in the preceding discourse while fail to persist as topics in the subsequent discourse. Specifically, 75% of the denotata of the preclauseal NPs in TOP are anaphoric, whereas only 27% persist as topics. These results differ from the results revealed in the present study because the method that Gregory and Michaelis adopts is different from mine. Their method of study is not imitated in my own study for two reasons: i) the way Gregory and Michaelis measures anaphoricity is different from the way they measure topic persistence; ii) their method of measuring topic persistence is not fit for measuring rightward discoursal associations of CIP topics in Chinese. The two reasons will be discussed in some detail below.

Gregory and Michaelis (ibid) regard anaphoricity as an index of the degree to which a referent can be claimed to have a discourse antecedent. It is scored on a value scale of 0-2 under different conditions. Tokens are scored "0" when the referents of preclausal NPs in them have not been mentioned in the preceding discourse. Tokens that contain preclausal NPs whose referents are members of a previously evoked set are scored "1". Tokens get "2" if preclausal NPs in them denote entities that have been previously mentioned. Tokens of the first type are easy to understand. Tokens of the second and third type are illustrated in the following examples used by Gregory and Michaelis:

(35) B: And because the parking brake hadn't been used in so many years, the pistons$_i$ froze up.
  A: Oh.
  B: So they ended up having to pound it out. And one of them$_i$ they were

able to get running, uh, kind of oiling it and playing with it and the
other one they just, it was just frozen solid...

(36) B: Right. [They go around in their little coaching shorts or—

A: Right, and a T-shirt.

B: —parachute pants]ᵢ

A: Right. Thatᵢ I didn't ever understand. I mean we've got coaches...

In (35), "one of them" is a member of the previously evoked set "the pistons" and
scored "1". Example (36) gets "2" because the preclausal NP "that" has a textual
antecedent. As for measure of topic persistence, the value scale of 0-2 is employed
in a different way. In Gregory and Michaelis, a token gets "0" if the preclausal NP
it contains is not referred to in the subsequent clauses. A token get "1" if the
preclausal NP it contains is referred to in the subsequent clauses by means of a
lexically headed NP. Lastly, a token is scored "2" if the preclausal NP it contains
is referred to in the subsequent clauses by a pronominal form. Instances where
tokens receive score "0" and "2" are easy to understand and will not be discussed
here. Instance of score "1" is cited as below from Gregory and Michaelis:

(37) A: Well [our house in New Mexico]ᵢ, itᵢ was stucco. But we had all this
trim to paint, and lots of it.

B: yeah.

A: And we did basically seventy-five percent of the houseᵢ and then I
was afraid to do the eves and high stuff.

The constituent "the house" is treated as the persistent form of "our house in New
Mexico". When the two sets of rules for scoring are compared, a gap between
them is discerned.

Table 6. 11 Gregory and Michaelis's Criteria for scoring preclausal NPs

Score	Anaphoricity (within 5 preceding clauses)	Topic persistence (within 5 subsequent clauses)	Consistency
0	Their referents have not been mentioned in the preceding discourse	Their referents are not referred to in the subsequent clauses	Yes

Score	Anaphoricity (within 5 preceding clauses)	Topic persistence (within 5 subsequent clauses)	Consistency
1	Their referents are members of a previously evoked set	Their referents are referred to in the subsequent clauses by means of a lexically headed NP.	?
2	Their referents denote entities that have been previously mentioned	Their referents are referred to in the subsequent clauses by a pronominal form	Yes

The question mark in the table indicates that the criteria for assigning score "1" to label anaphoricity and topic persistence are not entirely consistent since a member-of-set relation is involved in the identification of the former but not so in the latter. Instead, "a lexically headed NP" is set as a decisive factor for the identification of topic persistence valued at "1". This is shown in (37) where "the house" is a lexical repetition of "our house in New Mexico" and the two items have the same referent. As far as referent is concerned, it does not seem important to differentiate "a lexically headed NP" and "a pronominal form" and to score them differently when both are used as co-referring expressions. More importantly, zero form is not covered in the scaling system. This is the major reason why Gregory and Michaelis' criteria are not followed in this study. Consider:

(38) A: 这种巨大的变化是你们两位都没有曾经想到过的/
　　　B: R1 没有想到过/

From Gregory and Michaelis' perspective, the topic "这种巨大的变化" does not recur in the subsequent clause R1 and has no persistence. Since the verb phrase "想到" is a two-place predicate that takes two arguments, one playing the grammatical role of subject and the other object, the structure is still acceptable in Chinese when both arguments are dropped. If the two elements are added, clause R1 could be converted into one of the three forms (39b)~(39d) depending on the position the object occupies:

(39) a. 没有想到过/
　　　b. 这种巨大的变化我们没有想到过

147

c. 我们这种巨大的变化没有想到过
　　d. 我们没有想到过这种巨大的变化

There are no grounds for us to deny that clause (39a) is just a syntactic variation of any of the three instances. To ensure that all relevant data are captured in my study, variation of this type is ignored. The topic "这种巨大的变化" is simply interpreted as having rightward association with clause R1 regardless of whether the co-referring item is a zero form or a lexical form. Another case that expels Gregory and Michaelis' criteria is as follows:

　　(40) 这样的家世你是无法改变的/R1 这个历史你没有办法改写的/

Judging by Gregory and Michaelis' criteria, the topic "这样的家世" does not reappear literally in clause R1 and achieves no topic persistence. Nonetheless, the noun phrase is clearly paraphrased by "这个历史" in R1 and connected to it semantically. It hence esblishes discoursal association with R1. Such analysis reveals the discourse function of CIP topics to a fuller extent.

6.7　Summery

　　Based mainly on Halliday and Hasan's cohesion theory and Hoey' theory of lexis in text, CIP topics or elements contained in them are examined for their semantic connections. This makes feasible the measurement of their discoursal associations. Investigation of leftward and rightward associations provides a detailed picture of discourse features on the part of these clause-level constituents and reveals quantifiable relations holding between association and position. First, overall, CIP topics are more leftwardly associated than rightwardly associated in the corpus data. Namely, leftward associations surpass rightward ones. Second, to a large extent, the density of associations gradually drops on both sides of CIPT clauses when the position of associations changes from the point nearest to the topic structure to the point farthest away from it. Third, CIP topics exhibit a remarkably strong tendency to be discoursally associated in both directions and the two-way association pattern is prototypical. By contrast, one-way association pattern, either leftward only or rightward only, is infrequent and peripheral. Very rarely a CIP topic has no association in either direction within the scope of discourse chunk. It is safe to say that CIP topics are functionally motivated and manifest cognitive impetus. The discoursal properties on the part of CIP topics can be interpreted within the framework of spreading activation theory.

Chapter 7　Conclusion

7.1　Summary of major findings

　　Based on naturally occurring data collected from spoken Mandarin Chinese, this study is focused on clause-initial patient topics (CIP topics). It empirically investigates CIP topics at two levels—syntactic and discoual, and yields a series of findings that are briefly summarized in the space below.

　　As far as phrasal categories are concerned, linguistic units that can play the role of CIP topics are shown to be noun phrase, demonstrative, embedded clause, apposition construction, classifier phrase and verb phrase. These units exhibit a hierarchical tendency rather than an even one to be topicalized. Noun phrases are the most frequent in the corpus data and form the prototype while verb phrases are the most infrequent and peripheral. Within noun phrases, distinction is drawn between simple and complex noun phrases. The former far outnumber the latter. Analysis reveals that simple noun phrases are, short and brief in form, cognitively economic and facilitate information processing. This prompts them to occupy clause initial or near clause initial position to an overwhelming degree. Specifically, three subcategories of simple noun phrases—those that contain a demonstrative determiner, those that contain one modifier and bare nouns—tower above the others in terms of frequency. They hence become the prototypes both within the scope of noun phrases and the scope of pooled data. By contrast, complex noun phrases involve more linguistic materials and pose much cognitive burden for memory. Accordingly, they are restricted from occurring in TOP and make up only a small fraction of CIP topics. The same is true of apposition constructions and embedded clauses that are formally complex compared to simple noun phrases. At this point, Jin's view of Chinese language following a 'front-weight' principle is proved questionable. Demonstratives are singled out for examination in that they have rarely been touched upon in the literature in their capacity as topic. Moreover, units that contain a demonstrative determiner are shown to have a stronger tendency to occur in TOP than those that do not.

As for the syntax of topic structures that contain CIP topics, termed as CIPT clauses, the thesis extends the scope of study from the standard pattern TSV to non-standard ones so that more data are taken into consideration. This is proved to be necessary because many a CIPT clause of non-standard patterns is found to be convertible into clauses of TSV pattern. In all, four major syntactic types are identified in the corpus data, which can be divided into 22 subtypes, represented by 27 syntactic patterns. Two patterns are found to be prototypical: TSV and TV. They respectively make up 32.7% and 30.0% of the pooled data. Equivalence between TSV and OSV is tentatively depicted. A comparison is hence made between CIPT clauses in Chinese and topicalizations in English, drawing on Gregory and Michaelis' study for the English part. The occurrence of TSV clauses is shown to be 1.63 times as much as the occurrence of OSV clauses. A separate research on CIPT clauses based on data collected from two drama texts demonstrates that CIPT clause patterns identified in written Chinese are far less diverse than those found in spoken Mandarin. In this case, TV outnumbers TSV and becomes the prototype. According to an investigation into the English translations of those CIPT clauses, the occurrence of TSV clauses in the SL is 8.25 times as much as the occurrence of OSV translations in the TL. Evidently, the OSV construction is underused. The SVO construction is most frequently used in the TL, making up 52.2% of the data. Nonetheless, two problems are found with the SVO or SVOA/SVA translation in which the counterpart of a CIP topic is put in the post-verbal or post-prepositional position. First, the counterparts of CIP topics become the focus in the TL though the topics in the SL are not. Second, discoursal associations a CIP topic establishes in the original may fail to be retained or may even be weakened when the counterpart of topic occupies the clause-final or near-clause-final position.

Turning to discourse functions of CIP topics, the present study provides a detailed description of discoursal association patterns on the part of these topics. Within the scope of a discourse chunk, a topic or an element held in the topic may be semantically related to an element in a contextual clause by means of collocation, repetition, paraphrase or co-reference, etc. The topic hence acquires discoursal associations. Such associations are shown to figure more in positions adjacent to CIPT clauses than in positions distant from them. Namely, the nearer a position is to the CIPT clause, the more associations are in that position. This is true of associations on both left and right sides of CIPT clauses on a large scale. There are cases in which the two adjacent positions bear the same amount of associations. Yet, no case is found where associations in a position near to the topic structure are surpassed by those in a distant position. Further, distributions of leftward and rightward associations are not symmetric. On the whole, leftward associations surpass rightward ones. Associations in a given position on the left of CIPT clauses outnumber those in its symmetric position on the right, with few exceptions. Topic associations in relation to CIPT clause type exhibit consistent distributions. Noun phrase topics exhibit an association style surprisingly similar to that exhibited by CIP topics as a whole. For noun phrase topics that contain a demonstrative determiner, associations in position L1 tower over their counterparts in all the other sets of data. Noun phrase topics that contain a modifier exhibit a stronger tendency to be cataphoric than others do in terms of rightward associations. Bare noun topics exhibit anaphoricity and cataphoricity stronger than expected. Of the three patterns in which CIP topics are discoursally associated with contextual clauses—one exhibiting leftward and rightward associations simultaneously, one exhibiting leftward associations only and one exhibiting rightward associations only, the one showing associations in both directions predominates, accounting for 78.8% of the corpus data. The other two patterns are infrequent. The case in which a CIP topic has no association in either direction is rare and has only one occurrence. Cognitively, a CIP topic matches a node in the network of coherence in mentally-represented discourse. Its discoursal associations hence manifest the cognitive processes involved in speech production.

7.2 Implications

Though it is widely accepted that Chinese is a topic-prominent language, yet many of its features still remain uncovered when topic categorization is not taken into account. This study carries out an empirical research on CIP topics in spoken Mandarin. It extends from a syntactic examination to a discoursal one. The findings, judged from a broader angle, are therefore informative and have important implications.

First, following similar line of thoughts, future studies can be done on patient subtopics occupying a different position. Consider the example below：

(1) 我烈性酒从来不喝。（Xu and Liu 1998：61）

The topicalized noun phrase "烈性酒" occurs between the subject and predicate. Elements like this merit an independent investigation so that the syntactic and discoursal behavior of patient topics as a whole will be interpreted more accurately and systematically and that descriptions in this area will be as exhaustive as possible.

Second，research can be carried out in more specific ways focusing on a given category or subcategory of topics，like demonstrative topics，apposition construction topics or bare noun topics. Research can also be done on a specific subtype of CIPT clauses，especially clauses that contain the *shi. . . de* construction.

Third，other types of topics identified in Xu and Liu (1998)—domain topics, copy topics，clause topics—deserve similar explorations. Left dislocations can be examined in a similar way so that their distinct features are demonstrated in contrast with those of CIP topics.

Fourth，discoursal associations on the part of CIP topics and their distribution in written Chinese deserve examination to no less extent than those in spoken Chinese. Similar studies should also be done on other types of topics on the basis of written data so that clause topics in Chinese are investigated panoramically.

7.3 Limitations

What has been unveiled does not dwarf what remains to be unveiled. Even the unveiled aspects do not consummate the understanding of CIP topics in every way. For a start，though diverse syntactic patterns of CIPT clauses are found and depicted in chapter 5，still，there is a loophole. Consider：

(2) 这本书$_i$，读过$_i$的人不多。

The clause is cited from Xu and Langgendeon (1985) and Xu and Liu (1998：123). The topic binds the post-verbal gap within the relative clause in the comment. The entire clause will not be affected if the coreferential element "它" occurs in the post-verbal position. By intuition, the clause is quite acceptable and its occurrence should not be rare in spoken Mandarin. Yet, a topic structure of similar construction does not occur in my own corpus. On top of that, the rules followed in the present study to write out syntactic patterns of CIPT clauses fail to yield a description of the syntactic pattern of this clause. Clearly, the application of the rules is restricted. They do not apply when, as being shown in the above example, the element in TOP is governed by the verb phrase in a relative clause that premodifies an agent head.

Second, CIPT clauses often occur in a pair or bunch. If such a phenomenon could be analyzed as a whole in relation to the preceding or succeeding discourse, the study could produce a better explanation of the discoursal impetus for the occurrence.

Third, if an independent study were done on discoursal associations of objective constituents in clauses of SVO pattern, it would explain better the functional similarity or difference between topic and object.

Fourth, the prosodic features of CIP topics, CIPT clauses and topic markers are touched upon briefly where necessary. The results would be more revealing if the study could have been strengthened by essential means of acoustic equipment or software.

Bibliography

[1] Birner B. J. , G. Ward. 1998. Information Status and Noncanonical Word Order in English[M]. Amsterdam: John Benjamins.

[2] Bolinger D, D. A. Sears 1981. Aspects of Language[M]. New York: Harcourt Brace Jovanovich, Inc.

[3] Brown E. K. , J. E. Miller 1980. Syntax: A Linguistic Introduction to Sentence Structure[M]. Melbourne: Hutchinson Group Ltd.

[4] Brown G. , George Yule. 1983. Discourse Analysis [M]. Beijing: Foreign Language Teaching and Research Press. 2000.

[5] Carroll D. W. 1999. Psychology of Language[M]. Beijing: Foreign Language Teaching and Research Press. 2000.

[6] Chafe W. 1976. Giveness, Contrastiveness, Definiteness, Subjects, Topics and Point of View[A]. In C. N. Li (ed.) Subject and Topic[C]. New York: Academic Press, 25-56.

[7] Chao Yuen Ren(赵元任). 1968. A Grammar of Spoken Chinese[M].吕叔湘,译.汉语口语语法[M]. 北京:商务印书馆, 1979.

[8] Collins Allan M. , Elizabeth F. Loftus. 1975. A Spreading-Activation Theory of Semantic Processing[J]. Psychological Review 82:407-428.

[9] Croft W. 1990. Typology and Universals[M]. Beijing: Foreign Language Teaching and Research Press. 2000.

[10] Croft W. , D. A. Cruse. 2004. Cognitive Linguistics[M]. Beijing: Peking University Press. 2006.

[11] Downing P. 1995. Word order in discourse: by way of introduction[A]. In P. Downing and M. Noonan (eds.) Word Order in Discourse[C]. Amsterdam: John Benjamin, 1-28.

[12] Firbas J. 1992. Functional Sentence Perspective in Written and Spoken Communication [M]. 北京:世界图书出版公司,2007.

[13] Firth J. R. 1957. A synopsis of linguistic theory 1930-1955. In Studies in Linguistic Analysis[A]. Special edition of the Philological Society. In Liu Runqing et al. (eds.) Readings in Linguistics: Seventy-five Years since Saussure. Vol. II.

[14] 刘润清等编.现代语言学名著选读(下)[C].北京:测绘出版社,1988:85-120.

[15] Geluykens Ronald. 1992. From Discourse Process to Grammatical Construction: On Left-dislocation in English[M]. Amsterdam: John Benjamin.

[16] Gernsbacher M. A. , T. Givon. 1995. Introduction: Coherence as a mental entity[A]. In M. A. Gernsbacher & T. Givon (eds.) Coherence in Spontaneous Text[C]. Amsterdam:

John Benjamins, vii-x.

[17] Givon T. 1983. Topic Continuity in Discourse: An Introduction[A]. In T. Givon (ed.) Topic Continuity in Discourse: A Quantitative Cross-Language Study[C]. Amsterdam: John Benjamins, 1-41.

[18] Givon T. 1993a. English Grammar: A Function-based Introduction, Vol. I [M]. Amsterdam: John Benjamins.

[19] Givon T. 1993b. English Grammar: A Function-based Introduction, Vol. II [M]. Amsterdam: John Benjamins.

[20] Givon T. 1995a. Coherence in text vs. coherence in mind[A]. In M. A. Gernsbacher & T. Givon (eds.). Coherence in Spontaneous Text[C]. Amsterdam: John Benjamins, 59-115.

[21] Givon T. 1995b. Functionalism and Grammar[M]. Amsterdam: John Benjamins.

[22] Givon T. 2001a. Syntax: An Introduction, Vol. I[M]. Amsterdam: John Benjamins.

[23] Givon T. 2001b. Syntax: An Introduction, Vol. II[M]. Amsterdam: John Benjamins.

[24] Gregory M. L., L. A. Michaelis. 2001. Topicalization and Left-Dislocation: A Functional Opposition Revisited[J]. Journal of Pragmatics 33: 1665-1706.

[25] Gries S. T. 2004. Multifactorial Analysis in Corpus Linguistics: A Study of Particle Plancement[M]. Beijing: Peking University Press.

[26] Halliday M. A. K., R. Hasan. 1976. Cohesion in English[M]. London: Longman.

[27] Halliday M. A. K. 1994. An Introduction to Functional Grammar[M]. Beijing: Foreign Language Teaching and Research Press. 2000.

[28] Hoey M. 1983. On the Surface of Discourse[M]. London: George Allen & Unwin.

[29] Hoey M. 1991. Patterns of Lexis in Text[M]. Oxford: Oxford University Press.

[30] Hopper P. J., E. C. Traugott. 1993. Grammaticalization [M]. Beijing: Foreign Language Teaching and Research Press. 2001.

[31] Howard D. V. 1983. Cognitive Psychology: Memory, Language, and Thought[M]. New York: Macmillan.

[32] Hurford J. R., Heasley B. 1983. Semantics: A Coursebook[M]. Cambridge: Cambridge University Press.

[33] Jaszcaolt K. M. 2004. Semantics and Pragmatics: Meaning in Language and Discourse [M]. Beijing: Peking University Press.

[34] Keenan Elinor Ochs, Bambi B. Schieffelin. 1976. Topic as a Discours Notion: A Study of Topic in the Conversations of Children and Adults[A]. In Charles N. Li (ed.) Subject and Topic[C]. New York: Academic Press, 335-384.

[35] Kelly J., N. K. Mao. 2003. Fortress Besieged[M]. Beijing: Foreign Language Teaching and Research Press.

[36] Kim Kyu-hyun. 1995. WH-clefts and left-dislocation in English conversation[A]. In P.

Downing and M. Noonan (eds.) Word Order in Discourse[C]. Amsterdam: John Benjamins, 247-296.

[37] Krug Manfred G. 2001. Frequency, iconicity, categorization: Evidence from emerging modals[A]. In Joan Bybee & Paul Hopper (eds.) Frequency and the emegence of linguistic structure[C]. Amsterdam: John Benjamins, 309-335.

[38] Kurzon Dennis. 1988. The Theme in Text Cohesion[A]. In Yishai Tobin (ed.) The Prague School Legacy: In Linguistics, Literature, Semiotics, Folklore, and the Arts[C]. Amsterdam: John Benjamins, 155-162.

[39] Langacker R. W. 1991. Foundations of Cognitive Grammar Vol. I: Theoretical Prerequisites[M]. Beijing: Peking University Press. 2004.

[40] Langacker R. W. 1991. Foundations of Cognitive Grammar Vol. II: Descriptive Application[M]. Beijing: Peking University Press. 2004.

[41] LaPolla Randy J. Pragmatic relations and word order in Chinese[A]. In P. Downing and M. Noonan (eds.) Word Order in Discourse[C]. Amsterdam: John Benjamins, 297-329.

[42] Lappin S. (ed.) 1996. The Handbook of Contemporary Semantic Theory[M]. Oxford: Blackwell.

[43] Leech G. N., M. H. Short. 1981. Style in Fiction: A Linguistic Introduction to English Fictional Prose[M]. Beijing: Foreign Language Teaching and Research Press. 2001.

[44] Li C. N. (ed.) 1976. Subject and Topic[M]. New York: Academic Press.

[45] Li C. N., S. A. Thompson. 1976. Subject and Topic: A New Typology of Language[A]. In Charles N. Li (ed.) Subject and Topic[C]. New York: Academic Press, 457-490.

[46] Li C. N., S. A. Thompson. 1981. Mandarin Chinese: A Functional Reference Grammar [M]. Berkeley: University of California Press.

[47] McCarthy M., R. Carter, 1994. Language as Discourse: Perspectives for Language Teaching[M]. London: Longman.

[48] Palmer F. R. 1981. Semantics (Second Edition)[M]. Cambridge: Cambridge University Press.

[49] Pu Mingming. 1997. Zero Anaphora and Grammatical Relations in Mandarin[A]. In T. Givon (ed.) Grammatical Relations[C]. Amsterdam: John Benjamins, 281-321.

[50] Quirk R., S. Greenbaum, G. Leech, J. Svartvik. 1985. A Comprehensive Grammar of the English Language[M]. London: Longman.

[51] Radford A. et al. 1999. Linguistics: An Introduction [M]. Cambridge: Cambridge University Press.

[52] Radford A. 1997. Syntactic Theory and the Structure of English: A Minimalist Approach [M]. Beijing: Peking University Press. 2002.

[53] Robins R. H. 1989. General Linguistics[M]. London: Longman.

[54] Rossiter D., G. Lam, B. Mak. 2006. Automatic Audio Indexing and Audio Playback

Speed Control as Tools for Language Learning[A]. In Advances in Web Based Learning—ICWL[C], 290-299. Springer Berlin / Heidelberg.

[55] Scollon R., S. W. Scollon, A. Kirkpatrick. 2000. Contrastive Discourse in Chinese and English: A Critical Appraisal[M]. Beijing: Foreign Language Teaching and Research Press.

[56] Shi Dingxu. 2000. Topic and Topic-comment Constructions in Mandarin Chinese[J]. Language 76: 383-407.

[57] Shopen T. 1996. Language typology and syntactic description. Vol. I & II[M]. Cambridge: Cambridge University Press.

[58] Sperber D., D. Wilson. 1995. Relevance: Communication and Cognition (Second edition)[M]. Beijing: Foreign Language Teaching and Research Press. 2001.

[59] Tao Liang. 1996. Topic Discontinuity and Zero Anaphora in Chinese Discourse: Cognitive Strategies in Discourse Processing[A]. In Barbara Fox (ed.) Studies in Anaphora[C]. Amsterdam: John Benjamins, 487-513.

[60] Taylor John R. 1995. Linguistic Categorization: Prototypes in Linguistic Theory (Second edition)[M]. Oxford: Oxford University Press.

[61] Thornborrow J, Shan Wareing. 1998. Patterns in Language: Stylistics for Students of Language and Literature[M]. Beijing: Foreign Language Teaching and Research Press. 2000.

[62] Tsao Feng Fu(曹逢甫). 1977. A functional study of topic in Chinese: The first step towards discourse analysis[M]. 谢天蔚,译. 1995. 主题在汉语中的功能研究:迈向语段分析的第一步[M]. 北京:语文出版社.

[63] Ungerer F., H. J. Schmid. 1996. An Introduction to Cognitive Linguistics[M]. Beijing: Foreign Language Teaching and Research Press. 2001.

[64] Van Valin R. D., R. J. Lapolla. 1997. Syntax: Structures, Meaning and Function[M]. Cambridge: Cambridge University Press.

[65] Ward G. L., Ellen F. Prince. 1991. On the topicalization of indefinite NPs[J]. Journal of Pragmatics 16:167-177.

[66] Xu Liejiong, D. Terence Langendoen. 1985. Topic Structures in Chinese[J]. Language 61: 1-27.

[67] Yule George. 1996. Pragmatics[M]. Oxford: Oxford University Press.

[68] 巴金.家[M].曹禺改编.英若诚,译.1999,北京:中国对外翻译出版公司.

[69] 陈建民.1986,现代汉语句型论[M].北京:语文出版社.

[70] 陈平.1987,释汉语中与名词性成分相关的四组概念[A].1991,现代语言学研究——理论、方法与事实[C].重庆:重庆出版社,119-141.

[71] 陈平.1991,现代语言学研究——理论、方法与事实[M].重庆:重庆出版社.

[72] 陈平.1996,汉语中结构话题的语用解释和关系化[J].徐赳赳,译.国外语言学,4:27-36.

158

[73] 陈平.2004,汉语双向名词句与话题－陈述结构[J].中国语文,4:493-506.

[74] 范晓.1998,汉语的句子类型[M].太原:书海出版社.

[75] 范晓,胡裕树.1992,有关语法研究三个平面的几个问题[J].中国语文,4:272-278.

[76] 方经民.1993,现代语言学方法论[M].郑州:河南人民出版社.

[77] 方梅.2002,指示词"这"和"那"在北京话中的语法化[A].沈家煊.现代汉语语法的功能、语用、认知研究[C].商务印书馆,2005:255-282.

[78] 冯胜利.2000,汉语韵律句法学[M].上海:上海教育出版社.

[79] 高明乐.2004,题元角色的句法实现[M].北京:中国社会科学出版社.

[80] 耿素云,屈婉玲编.1990,集合论导引[M].北京:北京大学出版社.

[81] 顾阳.1994,论元结构理论介绍[J].国外语言学,1:1-11.

[82] 桂诗春编著.2000,新编心理语言学[M].上海:上海外语教育出版社.

[83] 桂诗春,宁春岩.1997,语言学方法论[M].北京:外语教学与研究出版社.

[84] 何向东主编.1999,逻辑学教程[M].北京:高等教育出版社.

[85] 胡裕树.1992,语法研究的三个平面[J].语文学习,11:36-38.

[86] 胡裕树主编.1995,现代汉语(重订本)[M].上海:上海教育出版社.

[87] 胡壮麟.1994,语篇的衔接与连贯[M].上海:上海外语教育出版社.

[88] 黄国文.1988,语篇分析概要[M].长沙:湖南教育出版社.

[89] 霍凯特.1958,现代语言学教程[M].索振羽,叶蜚声,译.1986,北京:北京大学出版社.

[90] 金积令.1991,英汉语主题结构的对比研究[J].外国语,2:1-7.

[91] 金积令.1998,汉语词序对比研究[J].外国语,1:28-35.

[92] 锦云.狗爷儿涅槃[M].英若诚,译.1999,北京:中国对外翻译出版公司.

[93] 老舍.茶馆[M].霍华,译.2001,北京:外文出版社.

[94] 李临定.1986,现代汉语句型[M].北京:商务印书馆.

[95] 廖秋忠.1986,现代汉语篇章中指同的表达[A].廖秋忠文集[C].1992,北京:北京语言学院出版社,45-61.

[96] 廖雅章.1988,从汉英句型对比看自然语言的普遍性[A].杨自俭,李瑞华主编.1990,英汉对比研究论文集[C].上海:上海外语教育出版社,481-495

[97] 刘丹青.2001,论元分裂式话题结构初探[A].徐烈炯,刘丹青主编.2003,话题与焦点新论[C].上海:上海教育出版社,220-241.

[98] 刘宓庆.2006,新编汉英对比与翻译[M].北京:中国对外翻译出版公司.

[99] 刘叔新.2002,现代汉语理论教程[M].北京:高等教育出版社.

[100] 刘叔新.2005,汉语描写词汇学[M].北京:商务印书馆.

[101] 刘顺著.2005,现代汉语语法的多维研究[M].北京:社会科学文献出版社.

[102] 陆俭明.1986,周遍性主语句及其他[A].陆俭明著.1993,现代汉语句法论[C].北京:商务印书馆,73-84.

[103] 陆俭明.2004,现代汉语语法研究教程[M].北京:北京大学出版社.

[104] 陆俭明,沈阳.2003,汉语和汉语研究十五讲[M].北京:北京大学出版社.

[105]　吕叔湘主编.1999,现代汉语八百词(增订版)[M].北京:商务印书馆.

[106]　吕叔湘,朱德熙.1980,语法修辞讲话[M].北京:中国青年出版社.

[107]　潘文国.1997,汉英语对比纲要[M].北京:北京语言大学出版社.

[108]　彭宣维.2000,英汉语篇综合对比[M].上海:上海外语教育出版社.

[109]　钱乃荣等.1990,现代汉语[M].北京:高等教育出版社.

[110]　钱钟书.1991,围城[M].北京:人民文学出版社.

[111]　邱述德,藏国芝.1994,话题－述题切分与语言结构[J].外国语,4:11-16.

[112]　屈承熹.2000,话题的表达形式与语用关系[A].徐烈炯,刘丹青主编.2003,话题与焦点新论[C].上海:上海教育出版社,1-29.

[113]　屈承熹.2006,汉语篇章语法[M].潘文国等,译,北京:北京语言文化大学出版社.

[114]　邵志洪,余继英.2006,汉英语言心理对比与翻译－TEM8(2005)汉译英试卷评析[J].中国翻译,1:78-81.

[115]　邵志洪,赵宏.2003,话题结构与主谓结构－话题语义类型与英译转换[J].解放军外国语学院学报,3:6-10.

[116]　沈家煊.1985,词序与辖域[A].杨自俭,李瑞华主编.1990,英汉对比研究论文集[C].上海:上海外语教育出版社,456-463.

[117]　沈家煊.1993,句法的象似性问题[J].外语教学与研究,1:2-8.

[118]　沈家煊.2000,导读,Croft W. 1990,Typology and Universals[M].北京:外语教学与研究出版社,F13-F25.

[119]　申小龙.1986,〈左传〉主题句研究[J].中国语文,2:130-142.

[120]　石定栩.1999,主题句研究[A].徐烈炯主编.1999,共性与个性－汉语语言学中的争议[C].北京:北京语言文化大学出版社,1-36.

[121]　石定栩.1999,"把"字句和"被"字句研究[A].徐烈炯主编.1999,共性与个性－汉语语言学中的争议[C].北京:北京语言文化大学出版社,111-138.

[122]　石定栩.2002,乔姆斯基的形式句法[M].北京:北京语言文化大学出版社.

[123]　施关淦.1991,关于语法研究的三个平面[J].中国语文,6:411-416.

[124]　施关淦.1992,八十年代现代汉语语法研究概说[J].中国语文,6:462-467.

[125]　石毓智,李讷.2001,汉语语法化的历程—形态句法发展的动因和机制[M].北京:北京大学出版社.

[126]　宋玉柱.1987,关于主谓谓语句的范围和类型[A].宋玉柱.1994,语法论稿[C].北京:北京语言学院出版社,209-218.

[127]　唐瑞琮.1987,古代汉语语法[M].沈阳:辽宁人民出版社.

[128]　童剑平.2009,汉语无标记名词短语句首受事话题及其特征研究[J].宁夏大学学报(社科版),3:35-39.

[129]　童剑平,程力.2009,汉语句首受事话题的语篇关联及其认知动因[J].东北师大学报(哲社版),1:96-100.

[130]　童剑平,周国强.2010,句首受事话题句及其英译[J].解放军外国语学院学报,4:81-86.

160

[131] 王桂珍.1996,主题、主位与汉语句子主题的英译[J].现代外语,4:46-50.

[132] 王力弟.2003,论元结构新论[M].北京:外语教学与研究出版社.

[133] 王寅.2003,认知语言学与语篇分析[J].外语教学与研究,2:83-88.

[134] 文炼.1991,与语言符号有关的问题—兼论语法分析中的三个平面[J].中国语文,2:83-88.

[135] 文旭.2005,左移位句式的认知解释[J].外国语,2:45-52.

[136] 吴惠荣,夏玉荣.2000,统计学原理[M].上海:上海交通大学出版社.

[137] 吴积才,程家枢编著.1981,现代汉语[M].昆明:云南人民出版社.

[138] 吴洁敏.1982,汉英语法手册[M].北京:知识出版社.

[139] 伍谦光.1988,语义学导论[M].长沙:湖南教育出版社.

[140] 武占坤主编.1985,现代汉语[M].石家庄:河北人民出版社.

[141] 吴中伟.2004,现代汉语句子的主题研究[M].北京:北京大学出版社.

[142] 肖俊洪.1992,从篇章的角度看游离宾语[J].外语学刊,6:17-23.

[143] 徐杰.2003,主语成分、话题特征及相应语言类型[J].语言科学,1:3-22.

[144] 徐赳赳.2003,现代汉语篇章回指研究[M].北京:中国社会科学出版社.

[145] 徐烈炯.1988,生成语法理论[M].上海:上海外语教育出版社.

[146] 徐烈炯,刘丹青.1998,话题的结构与功能[M].上海:上海教育出版社.

[147] 徐烈炯,刘丹青主编.2003,话题与焦点新论[M].上海:上海教育出版社.

[148] 徐烈炯.1999,名词性成分的指称用法[A].徐烈炯主编.1999,共性与个性－汉语语言学中的争议[C].北京:北京语言文化大学出版社,176-190.

[149] 许余龙.1992,对比语言学概论[M].上海:上海外语教育出版社.

[150] 许余龙.2004,篇章回指的功能语用研究[M].上海:上海外语教育出版社.

[151] 杨成凯.2000,汉语句子的主语和话题[A].徐烈炯,刘丹青主编.2003,话题与焦点新论[C].上海:上海教育出版社,51-82.

[152] 杨成凯.1997,"主主谓"句法范畴和话题概念的逻辑分析[J].中国语文,4:251-259.

[153] 袁毓林.1996,话题化及相关的语法过程[J].中国语文,4:241-254.

[154] 袁毓林.2003,汉语话题的语法地位和语法化程度[A].徐烈炯,刘丹青主编.2003,话题与焦点新论[C].上海:上海教育出版社,97-130.

[155] 袁毓林.2005,"都"的语义功能和关联方向新解[J].中国语文,2:99-109.

[156] 张宜生,张爱民.1996,汉语语序研究要略[J].江苏社会科学,3:109-112.

[157] 张志公主编.1982,现代汉语(中册)[M].北京:人民教育出版社.

[158] 赵艳芳.2000,认知语言学概论[M].上海:上海外语教育出版社.

[159] 郑超.2004,话题研究举疑[J].外国语言文学,1:10-14.

[160] 朱德熙.1982,语法讲义[M].北京:商务印书馆.

[161] 朱德熙.1985,语法答问[M].北京:商务印书馆.

[162] 朱永生,郑立信,苗兴伟.2001,英汉语篇衔接手段对比研究[M].上海:上海外语教育出版社.

Appendices

Appendix I List of CIPT clauses collected

Number	Token	Position
01.	人所有的就是他想要的	011623
02.	就是我所有的那种比如比较平等的关系，比较轻松的生活，就是我想要的	011628
03.	这个事其实当初就讨论过	011635
04.	我觉得可能文学的鉴赏力还是有一些吧	011955
05.	细节我不想多说	012159
06.	这个就很好解释了	013526
07.	这样是不能容忍的	013844
08.	两本书是同时写的	020553
09.	这个问题很多人问过	021300
10.	我们现在批判的东西˅你回头去看˅这个胡适的时代批评过	021407
11.	如果这些全部都知道的话	021500
12.	这种苦闷怎么样来解决	022446
13.	那个是在开始时候没有想到的	022946
14.	官章放下又走了	023150
15.	这种话不能自己来说	023300
16.	你就觉得某一步棋你要看见了	030516
17.	这听起来有点神奇	031023
18.	别的事情都不管	031840
19.	你的问题我不会做	032040
20.	嘉当是超越不了	032230

Number	Token	Position
21.	嘉当我比不上	032400
22.	他考虑了很久我知道	032720
23.	在芝加哥大学的退休制度我都没有参加	033040
24.	所有的"长"我都不做的	033250
25.	这个债你得还	033410
26.	别的不会想	034050
27.	这个最熟悉	034055
28.	他研究佛教的考据法至今没有人能够超越	040150
29.	国家的前途完全不知道	040650
30.	一二一游行很多学生都去参加了	040720
31.	这一点我得承认	041420
32.	之后所发生的一系列事情是汤一介万万没有想到的	041550
33.	她下放我并不知道	041610
34.	这种巨大的变化ᵛ是你们两位都没有曾经想到过的	041720
35.	这个问题应该讲ᵛ我是比较早的提出来的一个	042620
36.	认识史我们可不可以理解成为是人们对自身的认识和对世界的认识的这种变化发展的这种历史	042640
37.	那么仁义礼智的"仁"这个概念一提出来	042703
38.	那礼乐的思想跟仁到底有什么关系没有讲清楚	042708
39.	这种光彩我们在许多的大家的双眼当中都曾经看到过	043740
40.	那九个我们就带走了	050726
41.	他的机会也不会给你了	050755
42.	问题要让陈院长来解答	051640
43.	其他东西他们一般就不展出了	060140
44.	这个画过去的人研究得也很多了	060518
45.	谁也没有怀疑过这个画最初不是顾恺之画的	060530
46.	人物画是中国最早发展起来的一个画种	060908
47.	它这个山水画是后人临的也好	061015

Number	Token	Position
48.	两个底版一重叠	061336
49.	后宫里头就顾及不到	062510
50.	这个捍虎图啊画了不止一张	062925
51.	这首歌演唱得很有弹性	070500
52.	所有香港的比赛我都去参加	070545
53.	有人给你出唱片我们梦寐以求	070640
54.	失落肯定是有的	072330
55.	扑克牌我不会	080120
56.	麻将牌我不会	080124
57.	谁管谁我不知道	080129
58.	长袍马褂儿穿着	080530
59.	这样的考试您经历过几次	080730
60.	谁什么特征你都知道啊	080750
61.	这叫走心了	080755
62.	这纸什么时候捅破的也不知道	080810
63.	这纸什么时候捅破的也不知道	080810
64.	怎么捅破的不知道	080815
65.	历史的问题就历史解决吧	082030
66.	这个我们扔掉	090743
67.	这个服装为什么要改革呢	090808
68.	服装要改革	090830
69.	这个台湾有个很复杂的背景大家都知道	092222
70.	这是不能忽略的	092648
71.	历史上面已经存在的这种有地域特色的文化可能今天我们已经看不到了	092700
72.	文明戏你唱了以后	100910
73.	像横尸遍野ᵛ这个血流成河的这一种惨烈战争场面它几乎没有经历过	111730

Number	Token	Position
74.	这块砖多出来了以后呢	113050
75.	这块砖是绝对不能缺的一块砖	113102
76.	这块砖是绝对不能缺的	113120
77.	这个租界的生活现在是难以想象的	121003
78.	这一点人家都讲出来	121456
79.	这个档案还保存着	122205
80.	张爱玲他们根本不承认	122423
81.	比如散文∨散文写不完的	122445
82.	这条鱼他很难拉到岸上来	130512
83.	老妻子也没有	130936
84.	这我们都知道	131215
85.	宝玉已经找不到好长时间了	133300
86.	这个呢其他作品其实都还有	133449
87.	这么一种宏伟的内在结构是其他作品不太有的了	133455
88.	这话不能讲	140220
89.	什么事都要考虑到	140745
90.	这份赔偿协议是张伟主动提出来要签订的	141025
91.	上面还特别约定这个钱款都已经了结了	141250
92.	小霞受伤后的医疗费张伟都已结清	142210
93.	这个情况她是明知的	142255
94.	这几个条件叶志虎都符合吗	151815
95.	这句话有些人肯定不信	160130
96.	话虽这样说	160521
97.	一切材料购买齐备	160813
98.	这个他们都不管了	161020
99.	损失还没有补回来	161021
100.	装错房子这件事却很快在小区里传开了	161025

Number	Token	Position
101.	眼前的事情就算是处理完了	161440
102.	出这种事开发商也实在是想不到	162010
103.	钥匙能互开这样的事并没有签入合同	162117
104.	装错房子这样的事情完全是可以避免的	162340
105.	房子我们都住着	170234
106.	房产证是伪造的	170650
107.	这个道理王培君不可能不懂	170738
108.	房子又没地方去住	170835
109.	老房子早已拆迁	170840
110.	现在住的房子必须归还给房主	170846
111.	被骗走的钱一时半会儿又退不回来	170851
112.	她做这个事我真的是一点不知道	170930
113.	你跟其他人打交道我看也不要看	170942
114.	这个钱我还是还得出的	171016
115.	电话不接	171126
116.	而意外的是房门的锁也换掉了	171150
117.	她诈骗来的钱一部分拿去办出国手续了	171325
118.	剩下的也没用在家里	171331
119.	现在王培君的案子已经了结了	171532
120.	受害人在上当受骗后做出这样的猜测是完全可以理解的	171540
121.	但毕竟人家的不幸是自己的妻子一手造成的	171922
122.	现在窝都没有	172202
123.	集体财产ˇ你觉得该怎么分	180955
124.	这个账啊虽然是这样算	181155
125.	《电子园土地款分配方案》就此确定	181702
126.	1908 万元补偿款就已经发放完毕	181725
127.	我们镇里不能越权说,明确表态说这个土地款怎么分配	181816

Number	Token	Position
128.	把自己的村委会告上法庭 ᵛ 这是洪水坤不愿意看到的	181915
129.	我觉得这个事情我真的不想去做	190230
130.	那辆价值 300 万元的高档轿车 ᵛ 到底是怎么以 90 多万元、如此悬殊的价格卖出去的	190258
131.	现在车子不能交给你	190515
132.	这台车事实上就为你专门订的	190910
133.	这些损失是不是无法避免的呢	192445
134.	其余的他就不让我做了	200219
135.	这家务事外人还真的不太容易说得清	200312
136.	这孩子具体有没有我不清楚	200338
137.	这孩子具体有没有我不清楚	200338
138.	老婆孩子都没见过	200341
139.	你说 ᵛ 具体是姐姐还是妹妹我不大清楚	200352
140.	吕光华的工资一直是正常发放的	200524
141.	你对你父亲做的你觉得也是应该的	200649
142.	这就是要从法律上说了	200710
143.	这我也不知道	200715
144.	这搬迁手续也就一直没有办成	200720
145.	这事 ᵛ 还得从她的父亲吕光华去世之后不久说起	200850
146.	这份委托声明书的正文部分 ᵛ 并不是她自己亲笔写的	201250
147.	她的委托声明她都写错了	201305
148.	至于末尾那两句话,吕科华记得很清楚,当时是肯定写上去了	201348
149.	每一个字都是我写上的	201355
150.	后面的"共同参与,父亲所有遗产由大姑拥有,吕艳放弃继承"这些话全部都是吕科华利用这些空格后加的	201415
151.	那个老房子 ᵛ 如果要是卖的话	201730
152.	当时房屋拆迁还没有进行	201741
153.	搬迁这事是在 2004 年底就已经确定了	201800

Number	Token	Position
154.	量房子我不可能不知道	201817
155.	这个想法ˇ吕科华和吕艳他们双方都已经想到了	201831
156.	末尾两句话是后加的	201836
157.	我的语文水平一直提不高	210145
158.	那个专家不会翻	210340
159.	俄语专家他怎么知道版口这个词怎么说	210345
160.	这个……这个校对中间这些行话他不会说	210350
161.	《读书》杂志是很多老头办的	210608
162.	功劳都应该记在这些老头身上	210612
163.	所谓"读书无禁区"也是那个时候《读书》提出来的	210640
164.	这个要不要发	211008
165.	这篇文章就退了	211021
166.	什么话别人都不说	211450
167.	丁先生大家都熟	212020
168.	那这话谁说呢	220709
169.	这个匾额写好了	221309
170.	名字都考证出来了	222413
171.	就是乾隆初期这个书就写好了	222635
172.	像元迎探惜ˇ她们都是有可能选进宫的。	231005
173.	这个元春呢ˇ小说就告诉你就选进去了	231010
174.	这个"逗漏"两个字啊希望你注意	231230
175.	这点写错了呀	231350
176.	这个事情我在前几回里面讲过	231525
177.	清虚观打醮的发起者是贾元春ˇ书里面是非常清楚地给我们写出来的	231555
178.	那这一笔我想曹雪芹他不会是乱写	231650
179.	曹雪芹的《红楼梦》里每句话他都是认真下笔	231700
180.	这样的家世你是无法改变的	232045

Number	Token	Position
181.	这个历史你没有办法改写的	232050
182.	这个就不清楚	232110
183.	这个写得没有道理呀	232435
184.	秦可卿的丧事都办完了	232450
185.	这个话实际上是生活当中曹家人当时说过的话	233330
186.	这个木料原来是谁定的货呀	243357
187.	这个樯木呢是这样的人物才能使用的	243500
188.	这个事情我不要再公开讨论，	251604
189.	这个你这房子情况我也看了	260850
190.	不妥当的话　不妥当的事,你们尽量少说少做	261050
191.	房子给了小儿子	270433
192.	毕业证书他也没有	271730
193.	连一个中学毕业证书都没有	271740
194.	每天大概二三十块钱也能挣得到	271900
195.	其他事情我也不会	271930
196.	这起家庭纠纷最后该如何解决呢	272215
197.	老父亲的遗产黄家兄妹七人均有权依法继承	272330
198.	他的义务他没有切实地履行	272345
199.	我们追到他连云港,连云港老家我们都去了	280520
200.	但我后面是谁我没去看	290410
201.	这个画像很顺利就画出来了	290552
202.	他用他名字用他的绰号所那个登记的房屋他不住	291308
203.	机关它就不邀请了	300503
204.	至于背后的犯罪呢它无权更好地查处	300929
205.	重大问题你政府不邀请	301313
206.	你比如河北唐山开平区刘官屯煤矿的12·7重大责任事故ˇ这个案件那么我们挂牌督办	302330
207.	有的话他也好像还不太明白	310600

Number	Token	Position
208.	孩子就交给你了	310740
209.	这些话往往都是刚入行不久的新老师才这么说	310944
210.	这些话你都不许说	311610
211.	这个影响可能是没有爱心、缺乏爱心的老师可能他不会预料到的	312332
212.	这个我相信	320242
213.	所谓"丁克"这个词当然是从国外引进的	320414
214.	那社会上更多的公益事情其实他可以去关注	321130
215.	这个现在已经逐渐在做	321201
216.	养老院这个制度能不能推行开	321218
217.	这个新手实际上还没有完全培养出来	331520

Appendix II List of data sources

Number	Data source	Recording time/ Length(ms)	Genre	TV program
01.	李银河:性学前沿的女行者	040316 - 45	对话	CCTV 10:百家讲坛
02.	龙应台:文人做官	040318 - 45	对话	CCTV 10:百家讲坛
03.	几何学家:陈省身	031221 - 45	对话	CCTV 10:大家
04.	汤一介:不知疲倦的思想者	040411 - 40	对话	CCTV 10:大家
05.	走出红土地	050505 - 20	谈话	SHTV 纪实:往事
06.	文物鉴定家杨新:古画探源	060203 - 40	对话	CCTV 10:大家
07.	张明敏的中国心	060203 - 25	介绍、讲述	CCTV 10:讲述
08.	文物鉴定家耿宝昌:人间国宝	060204 - 38	对话	CCTV 10:大家
09.	葛剑雄主讲:地域文化	051125 - 40	讲座	CCTV 10:百家讲坛
10.	"369"说滑稽:访杨华生	050502 - 20	对话	SHTV 纪实:往事
11.	大漠雄关 - 嘉峪关	031122 - 50	谈话	CCTV 10:家园

Number	Data source	Recording time/ Length(ms)	Genre	TV program
12.	张爱玲	031212－30	介绍、讲述	CCTV 10：人物
13.	余秋雨主讲：文学创作中的未知结构	040218－42	讲座	CCTV 10：百家讲坛
14.	结婚前的一场意外	060214－27	介绍、讲述	CCTV12：经济与法
15.	砍柴的遭遇	060215－32	介绍、讲述	CCTV 12：经济与法
16.	谁装修了我的新房	060215－30	介绍、讲述	CCTV 12：经济与法
17.	诈骗案后案	060217－25	介绍、讲述	CCTV 12：经济与法
18.	难分的巨款	060220－26	介绍、讲述	CCTV 12：经济与法
19.	没有赢家的买买	060220－30	介绍、讲述	CCTV 12：经济与法
20.	精神病人的遗产	060222－25	介绍、讲述	CCTV 12：经济与法
21.	沈昌文	031213－30	介绍、讲述	CCTV 10：读书时间
22.	阎崇年主讲：清十二帝疑案(乾隆上)	051125－42	讲座	CCTV 10：百家讲坛
23.	刘心武主讲：贾元春原型之迷	050917－40	讲座	CCTV 10：百家讲坛
24.	刘心武主讲：秦可卿出身之谜	050514－40	讲座	CCTV 10：百家讲坛
25.	物理学家－杨振宁	060325—28	介绍、讲述	CCTV 10：人物
26.	和为贵－同一个屋檐下	060307－28	介绍、讲述	CCTV 12：经济与法
27.	父亲的秘密	060321－28	介绍、讲述	CCTV 12：经济与法
28.	疑案5·19下集：三滴血	060326—20	介绍、讲述	CCTV 12：第一线
29.	神偷落网记	060327－24	介绍、讲述	CCTV 12：第一线
30.	让"铁腕"真正硬起来	060328－25	介绍、谈话	CCTV 新闻：央视论坛
31.	别让话语伤着孩子	060217－24	介绍、谈话	CCTV 新闻：央视论坛
32.	当独生子女成为父母	060429－23	介绍、谈话	CCTV 新闻：央视论坛
33.	耍孩儿戏	040228－25	介绍、讲述	CCTV 新闻：文化报道

后　记

　　本书基于笔者的博士学位论文内容修改补充而成。除了对文字、数据进行校对、个别之处修改并增加缩略语、符号的汉语解释，全书总体保持了原论文的风格。在本书出版之际，我要感谢很多人。

　　衷心感谢我的导师、上海交通大学外国语学院周国强教授。周国强教授在我撰写博士论文过程中的悉心指导和严格要求令我在学识上长进、收获甚丰；他对待学生们平易近人、谦和真诚的风范更令我在品格修养上所学颇多。同时也由衷感谢师母在我遇到困难时给予我的关心、帮助。上海交通大学郑树棠教授、刘龙根教授、胡全生教授、陈永捷教授、陈德民教授、胡开宝教授、朱振才教授、华东师范大学潘文国教授、华东理工大学邵志洪教授对我的博士论文都提出了宝贵的修改意见，在此深表谢意。感谢雷秀云博士、阚哲华博士、姜孟博士、王奇博士、张莹博士、王勇博士、林伟杰博士对我的支持和帮助。

　　还要感谢我的家人给予我的理解和支持。